By Barry Michels and Phil Stutz

The Tools: 5 Tools to Help You Find Courage, Creativity and Willpower—and Inspire You to Live Life in Forward Motion

Coming Alive: 4 Tools to Defeat Your Inner Enemy, Ignite Creative Expression & Unleash Your Soul's Potential

COMING ALIVE

COMING ALIVE

4 TOOLS TO DEFEAT YOUR
INNER ENEMY, IGNITE
CREATIVE EXPRESSION &
UNLEASH YOUR SOUL'S
POTENTIAL

Barry Michels
& Phil Stutz

Spiegel & Grau
New York

Copyright © 2017 by Barry Michels and Phil Stutz

Published in the United States by Spiegel & Grau, an imprint of Random House, a division of Penguin Random House LLC, New York.

SPIEGEL & GRAU and Design is a registered trademark of Penguin Random House LLC.

LIBRARY OF CONGRESS CATALOGING-IN-PUBLICATION DATA
Names: Michels, Barry, author. | Stutz, Phil, author.
Title: Coming alive : 4 tools to defeat your inner enemy, ignite creative expression & unleash your soul's potential / Barry Michels and Phil Stutz.
Description: First edition. | New York : Spiegel & Grau, [2017]
Identifiers: LCCN 2017013595 | ISBN 9780812994117 | ISBN 9780812994124 (ebook)
Subjects: LCSH: Self-actualization (Psychology) | Change (Psychology)
Classification: LCC BF637.S4 S8485 2017 | DDC 158—dc23
LC record available at https://lccn.loc.gov/2017013595

Hardcover ISBN 978-0-8129-9411-7
International edition ISBN 978-0-399-59118-1
Ebook ISBN 978-0-8129-9412-4

Printed in the United States of America on acid-free paper

randomhousebooks.com
spiegelandgrau.com

987654321

First Edition

Book design by Donna Sinisgalli
Illustrations by Ryan Noetzel

To Judy White, who, like Daphne becoming the laurel, dared me to become the wind

—Barry Michels (with help from Rainer Maria Rilke)

For Andrew, who faced death as a boy and in the struggle became a man

—Phil Stutz

"To live is the rarest thing in the world. Most people exist, that is all."

—OSCAR WILDE

"Awake, arise, or be for ever fallen!"

—JOHN MILTON, *PARADISE LOST*

CONTENTS

COMING ALIVE

Introduction

Most people suspect they could live a completely different life from the one they're now living. In this other life their days are joyful. They're more confident, they take more risks, the things they do feel more meaningful. It's as if—in this alternate existence—they've plugged into a different kind of energy, an energy that makes anything seem possible.

What they suspect is true. This energy is real and it has the power to change lives. We call it the Life Force. It's the great prize of the universe—immortal, unstoppable, endlessly creative.

Most of us have experienced the Life Force in some way. You may have felt it at the birth of a child. It might have emerged as an urge to play an instrument that you gave up on when you were younger. Maybe you were stuck on something you were writing and then suddenly the solution came to you out of nowhere. Or perhaps you felt a dizzying grace when members of your family treated one another with love.

There are an endless number of examples, each one reflecting the guiding, creating, infinitely nurturing qualities of the Life Force.

The most significant use of the Life Force is that it allows each of us to put our stamp on the world, to give it something that is uniquely our own. It doesn't matter if it's something huge and public or something humble and private, as long as it's meaningful to you. When you use the Life Force in this way, you feel fully alive.

But most of us get no more than a quick glimpse of this other life before a curtain drops and we lose touch with it—wondering if it ever really existed. We find ourselves back in tedious "normal" life—stripped of promise, focused on what we can't do, not on what we can. The source of our powerlessness, we believe, is some painful personal problem we are unable to overcome. It doesn't matter what the problem is—what matters is that you're unable to conquer it.

Here are some of the ways our patients describe problems they've been unable to vanquish. Do any of these statements sound familiar to you? Do they apply to you or someone in your life?

I can't control my thoughts. I scan my life looking for things to worry about. It's like I'm torturing myself.

I feel like there's this in-group I can never be a part of. It's like there's something wrong with me. When I'm around people my mind fills with negative thoughts about myself.

I can't stand up to my boyfriend because I'm too afraid of losing him. On nights when I'm not with him I drive past his house to make sure he's not out with someone else.

I feel overwhelmed by the amount I have to get done, yet I sit in front of the TV like a zombie. I don't know what I'm waiting for.

The world is unfair. People don't treat me the way I deserve. When my feelings are hurt I don't get over it for days.

The nature of the problem is different for each of these people. But they have one thing in common: their problems seem insurmountable. Going to therapy and understanding the "cause" of the problem is no guarantee they can solve it—what we've found (after a combined seventy years of experience as practicing psychotherapists) is that "understanding" isn't the key to overcoming emotional problems.

So what is? Hidden behind each problem is a force working to make sure you don't solve it. When you can't overcome an emotional problem you feel powerless, and getting what you want from life feels impossible. This sense of impossibility keeps spreading—a poison in your soul. Eventually you give up on expressing who you really are, on living the way you suspect you could.

Being unable to solve your personal problems isn't an indicator of lack of potential. It's a sign that a powerful adversary is blocking your access to the Life Force.

But concepts and theories won't give you access to the Life Force. You can't think yourself back to life. To free yourself, you need to *feel* the forces of life as they flow through you.

So how do you access the Life Force? You need tools. Imagine a can of soup. If you want to know what the soup tastes like, reading the side of the can won't help; you need to actually taste it. Unless you have the hand strength of a superhero, this is impossible without a can opener.

Think of this book as a can opener for your soul. It will give you the tools you need to access the Life Force and defeat your inner enemy. Only then will you discover what you're truly capable of and come alive in a way you never have before.

Chapter One

Reclaiming Your Life

Phil exposes the inner enemy that traps you in a limited existence, and guides you through the first steps toward activating your full potential.

HOW I CAME ALIVE

I BECAME AWARE OF THE POWER OF THE LIFE FORCE as a college student—but it wasn't part of my course work. At seventeen, I was already in my sophomore year. Physically and emotionally immature, I belonged back in high school. During my freshman year I had indulged my greatest love—basketball. When I was sixteen years old, I played on the best freshman team the school had had in years.

Now I wanted to move up to the varsity. I wasn't ready. I needed to wait a year and get bigger and stronger. But I was a gym-rat whose pulse would quicken at the sound of the bouncing ball. I made the team—barely—and then I got what I deserved. I spent the next two years "riding the pine."

(The pine was the wooden bench the scrubs sat on during games.)

Worse than not playing was the dismissive way the coach treated the scrubs. By the time I was a senior, my confidence was destroyed. But what happened in that final season prepared me for the future in a way I never could have anticipated.

The team was even better than when I was a freshman. The best player was an All-American point guard. I was his substitute, which meant I only played when he was injured or had fouled out—usually when the score was close and the crowd was going berserk.

If I sat inertly watching, by the time I entered the game I'd be so cold I could barely move. So I'd "put myself in the game" from the bench. I'd jump up and down, scream at the top of my lungs, yell out where the screens were, etc. Besides keeping me loose, it had an effect I didn't anticipate—it lifted up the energy of the guys actually playing.

The best moments were when my excitement spread to the rest of the team. I learned that I could inspire others to do things they'd never done before. It was at those moments that I felt most alive. What I didn't realize at the time was that I was being prepared for my future.

RECOGNIZING THE LIFE FORCE

Winning was great, but the most alive part of the experience—the part I still remember fifty years later—was feeling that inner fire grow. The more powerful the other team, the more difficult the challenge, the more inspired we became. The drive to experience this inspired state is what moves competitive athletes to train for hours every day.

But sports are just one place to discover untapped potential. As a psychiatrist, my job isn't to win basketball games, it's to help people discover what they're capable of. This happens in obvious ways, like helping them get a better job, be a stronger leader, or break through a creative block. But our most important potentials aren't so obvious: to give and receive love, to listen to other people, to accept what life brings, to be patient—the spiritual and emotional abilities that work inside us and are the essence of what it means to be human. If you were building a fire, they would be the ring of stones that holds in the fire's heat, allowing the flames of inspiration to grow and connect you to what I came to call the Life Force.

The Life Force speaks constantly—not in words, but through events. You can feel it as an undeniable *presence* guiding you. More commonly, you'll feel its presence for brief moments, usually in reaction to a deeply moving event: the birth of a child, the act of falling in love, or a trip to a faraway place that awakens something deep within you.

Or it can emerge without explanation as a sudden insight into another person, as the solution to a problem that's defeated you for months or as a burst of creative expression that comes from somewhere beyond you. These moments of inspiration can seem random, but they're reminders that the Life Force is always there.

But knowing the Life Force is there isn't enough if you don't know how to connect to it. Look around. The people you see living inspired, expansive lives are the exceptions.

The vast majority of human beings are caught in limited, joyless lives—every attempt to change seems thwarted.

Maybe you're a songwriter with an idea for a film script. Rather than becoming excited about writing in a new medium, it feels beyond you and you give up. Or maybe you've developed strong feelings for a person you've always thought of as a friend, but when you're around him you automatically close yourself off. Or perhaps you've run a lot of 5Ks and you'd like to run a marathon, but you're not willing to commit to the time it takes to train for one.

All of these people want to open a new door in their lives, but the door is locked. There is only one key: the Life Force itself. But we've forgotten how to find the Life Force. In so doing, we've *lost the key to our own future.* How could we lose something so priceless?

Because we look for it in the wrong place. In our consumer culture, we look outside ourselves for everything. Products are sold with the claim they will magically solve life's problems. The right hair conditioner will attract the perfect mate. The right wristwatch will give you the aura of success. A new car, a new lover, or a new home may create temporary excitement—but it doesn't last. Like a child excitedly playing with a Christmas present he's just unwrapped, we quickly lose interest and move on to another gift.

This fixation on things outside of us makes change impossible. If you want to open the door to a future with real potential, you'll need to access the *inner* power of the Life Force. You won't be able to see it, you can't hold it in your hand, but when it's flowing through you it will inspire you to do things you didn't think were possible.

THE LIFE FORCE IN HISTORY, NATURE, AND PEOPLE

The belief that an invisible animating energy underlies our existence is thousands of years old. Unlike our modern, mechanical notion of energy, which we understand via mathematics, this is a living energy that we feel inside us. In Eastern religions, this energy, or Life Force, is known variously as *prana* (in Indian philosophy and medicine), *lung* (in Tibetan Buddhism), and *chi* (in Chinese philosophy and medicine). In the Old Testament, it was called *ruach*, the breath of God, which gave mankind not only life, but the spirit to evolve.

The Life Force itself may be invisible, but evidence of its power is everywhere. It created life on earth and, over untold eons, drove evolution from single-cell organisms to the unimaginable complexity of the human brain. Every seed that sprouts into a full-grown plant, every salmon that fights its way against the current to spawn, every sun-seeking weed growing through cracks in the sidewalk, is an expression of life's unstoppable energy.

How does this affect you as an individual? The songwriter, lovesick friend, and runner were stuck; maybe they'd failed so many times they lost hope that change was possible. No amount of talking or analyzing could free them from their dark conclusions. But the Life Force affects you in a way that thinking can't. You can *feel* its inspiring presence. When you do, you experience a force that has sustained all living forms for millions of years.

It's natural to think of the Life Force as sustaining growth in nature—the grass growing, fish swimming, birds flying, etc. But the Life Force is capable of something more: it can fuel the inner growth of each of us. When you learn how to use its energy it becomes the antidote to the personal problems that fill us with a sense of powerlessness.

Every human being is blessed with the ability to use the Life Force in this way, but unlike its workings in nature, harnessing its power for inner growth requires a conscious choice.

YOU MUST CHOOSE TO INSPIRE YOURSELF

Making this choice in your head isn't enough; you register your choice through *action*. Living a life filled with unstoppable passion doesn't happen by itself; it requires a heightened Life Force, and that takes work. Many times we build our Life Force without realizing what we're doing. When I was screaming at my teammates from the bench it didn't occur to me that I was stimulating their collective Life Force. But the more I did it, the more familiar it became, until it became a ritual I looked forward to.

Athletes in every sport, on every level, have rituals designed to stimulate their Life Force. Observe the players' rituals before a game. The hopping, bouncing, slapping, and bumping might look like an overly aggressive dance number, but actually is a celebration of the Life Force.

Athletics isn't the only arena that benefits from an expanded Life Force. Any role that requires you to lead, to create, or to perform—an actor, a lawyer in court, a teacher, etc.—benefits from a strong Life Force.

The most universal practice for tapping into the Life Force

is really a number of practices—meditation, prayer, reading, journal writing, exercise—that make up the morning rituals that so many people swear by. Rather than preparing you for a single event, like a game, a play, or a public address, the rituals prepare you for the entire day to come.

Every time you "practice" these activities—all of them or a select few—you are making the "choice" to apply the Life Force to your own growth.

THE GUY WITH THE GUN

If choosing to trigger the Life Force is an action that anyone can take, each of us is free to bring this power into his or her life. But remarkably, even when we know it's available to us, *we don't activate it.* Instead we make a choice that makes us weaker: we give up on something out of laziness, avoid social situations out of insecurity, yell at a subordinate for an unavoidable business setback. We look back in wonder and ask, "Why did I do that? What was I thinking?" And the most disturbing question: *"Why do I keep making this choice over and over?"* The answer is that these weren't choices any more than you have a choice when a mugger puts a gun to your head and tells you to empty your pockets.

The "guy with the gun" is forcing you to make the choice *he* wants you to make, not the choice that connects you to life. His goal is to deaden you and take away your freedom and your future. He doesn't want your money; he wants your passion, your inspiration, your potential—all for himself.

The guy with the gun is a symbol, but of what? It would

have to be something of immense power, strong enough to make you repeat the same choices *even after you realize how bad they are for you.*

We think of ourselves as rational beings with good reasons for the things we do. The last thing we want to admit is that a force we're not aware of is making decisions for us. Especially one that has an agenda that is completely at odds with the way we want to live.

But admit it or not, this "other" force is real. It's more than the result of psychological damage, though that makes its effects stronger. Present from birth, it's an irrational force built into every human being. It's a part of me, you, and everyone else.

Its presence doesn't mean there's anything wrong with you. It's not an illness, nor is it a punishment. But it's always there, and every commitment you don't keep, every challenge you avoid facing, every impulse you give in to, is the work of this force. When you wake up at 4 a.m. worried about paying your mortgage, when you hate someone so much you can't concentrate on your own work, when you've been publicly humiliated and think the whole world is laughing at you, you are seeing the world through the eyes of this force.

A TIME OF GREAT PROMISE

I was thrown in the path of this inner enemy when I least expected it. I had just finished my psychiatric residency. Years of training now complete, I finally had what I most craved—freedom. For me, freedom didn't mean traveling the world, it meant treating patients the way my instincts told me to.

This was a time of great promise. I was feeling the excitement that comes with doing what you are meant to do in life. It doesn't take much to start a psychiatric practice—just an office. But I was missing one other crucial ingredient—experience. I was about to get it.

In a profession known for the silent reserve of its practitioners, I stood out like a sore thumb. I didn't look at therapy the way my peers did. They saw the patient as "ill," and their job was to "cure" them. This was the standard psychiatric model, and I rejected this almost as soon as it was taught to me. When you treat a person like they're a "case," it puts them at a distance. You can't close that gap by asking a million factual questions; you need to connect with their experience through your heart.

My guiding star wasn't psychiatry—it was basketball. That's where I'd developed my passion for helping others reach their potential. In that context, success wasn't some final end point, it was a commitment to constant growth. The range of human potential is limitless: anything from playing an instrument to becoming a leader in your community to discovering a new path to spirituality to learning to be vulnerable with your spouse—all are within your grasp.

As different as these potentials are from one another, they have one thing in common—to my patients they felt out of reach. I didn't feel that way. To me, overcoming the seemingly impossible is the essence of being alive. My job was to make that a real experience for my patients.

Some of my peers accused me of going off on a tangent and pursuing some starry-eyed goal while doing nothing to "treat the illness" my patients were suffering from. The opposite was true. When a patient commits to pursuing their potential, it triggers their Life Force, and *it's the Life Force that gives them the vitality to heal themselves.* You can bury your symptoms with meds, you can avoid situations that trigger them, but if you want to change yourself in a lasting way, you need to put yourself in forward motion and pursue your potential.

The further I could take a patient toward realizing their potential, the more satisfying it was for me. The most exciting thing was when someone discovered an ability they *didn't even know they had.* It was the ultimate victory, a mystical experience as powerful as being present at the birth of a child. It was so satisfying I sometimes felt guilty that I was getting paid to witness it.

Patients developed these hidden abilities more often than you'd imagine. But you can't develop potential until you discover what you have potential for. I found an "instrument" inside myself that could pick up the existence of potential talent before the patient could—it was my own passion.

What I'd developed playing basketball in college—my wild enthusiasm to see others transcend their limits—hadn't gone away. As a therapist, I discovered it did more than inspire patients, it let me uncover their hidden abilities. My passion, the all-out commitment to my patients' growth, was like a flashlight illuminating parts of them they weren't aware of.

FORCE VERSUS COUNTERFORCE

Thrilled at what I was learning and pleased that I was getting referrals, I thought I was off to a great start. I assumed that my enthusiasm would get me through every situation. Because I was a rank beginner, nothing had yet happened to contradict that delusion. But enthusiasm wasn't enough to meet the opponent I was about to face.

Most new patients define progress in terms of symptoms. That's natural because it's their symptoms—depression, panic attacks, obsessions, insomnia, etc.—that bring them to therapy in the first place. My practice being young, most of my patients were new to therapy; new patients often make quick progress, especially when they get infected with my enthusiasm.

But before I got completely carried away with my own brilliance, something happened that disturbed and confused me. *Their symptoms came back.* It didn't seem to matter what the symptoms were—constant worry, avoidance of intimidating situations, insecurity in public, inability to commit in a relationship—they all resurfaced.

Sometimes it was dramatic. Someone working on their rage and frustration would find themselves screaming at other drivers and instigating arguments. Another person would go on creative strike, and rather than work on something they were writing, they'd plop down in front of the TV for hours. Someone working on a business start-up would give in to a chronic gambling habit.

Sometimes it was banal. A person trying to lose weight would eat that one extra piece of cake. An executive would arrive ten minutes late to his own meetings. A wife would project an almost imperceptible coolness each time she walked past her husband. While these symptoms may be small, their long-term effects can cause the loss of a marriage, a career, or physical health.

Regardless of what problem my patients had, they were suddenly no closer to its solution than when they started therapy. Caught up in my enthusiasm, they'd become hopeful that they could free themselves from the pain and limitations making them miserable. Those hopes were now shattered. I'd try to restart the engine, pouring as much enthusiasm as I could muster back into my patients. But I was talking off the top of my head; I had no idea why these failures were happening.

The reaction of my patients stung. In one instance, a patient wanted to marry a woman he loved, but had problems with erections and was afraid to commit to her. All his tests were normal; it was a "psychological" issue. Initially caught up in my enthusiasm, he was able to overcome the problem. He proceeded to buy her a ring. But the improvement was temporary, and his sexual problems returned. He felt tricked, and he wasn't shy about telling me.

"I've committed to a marriage that doesn't work. You're a great salesman but I don't think you know how to help people."

He was right that I didn't help him, but it definitely wasn't for lack of serious commitment. Helping him was impossible because I didn't understand the force I was up against. In physics, a "force" has the power to make an object change course. In human psychology, there is a force that has the power to make *you* change course—just the way a guy with a gun to your head could. And what direction does this force push you in? It's to act against growth, against forward motion, against your evolution.

If the Life Force opens limitless potential in all of us, this opponent is its *counterforce*, destroying your potential and casting you down into a life of limitation. It makes its presence known through rage, impulsivity, addiction, laziness, panic, negativity, and so on. What's most striking is that you keep doing these things even though you know how bad they are for you. You give in to a sugar binge, or you instigate a shouting match at a family dinner, and after it's over you ask yourself, "Why do I keep doing this?"

The fact that you're asking the question says that you're not yet aware of the counterforce. Just as gravity makes flying impossible, this inner opponent makes growth impossible. Its signature isn't one incident of self-destructive behavior, it's that you repeat the behavior over and over. It's the equivalent of beating your head against the wall. When I began to identify the counterforce working in my patients, I was naïve enough to believe I could convince them with words to "stop being so self-destructive."

I might as well have tried to convince them to fly without an airplane. No matter how determined I was to change their lives, this opposing force was just as determined to keep them stuck. And that force felt *stronger* than I was. I was in a wrestling match with an invisible opponent so powerful he could pin me to the mat and never let me up.

The physical presence of a crushing, hindering force as the real cause of my patients' symptoms was outside what I'd been taught in my training. Psychiatrists think in theoretical terms; this didn't feel any more theoretical than a brick falling on your head. The more I faced this force and felt its presence, the more convinced I became that it was something real.

I had completed my training but, like most young psychiatrists, I still had a supervisor I'd see to discuss my cases. The supervisor I chose was informal, maybe ten years older than I was, and very supportive. If there was anyone I could talk to openly about the experiences I was having, it would be him.

I asked him if he'd ever felt a destructive force in his patients that was more than just a theory, something that was so intense it felt real. He gave me an "It's time to grow up" smile that immediately told me he put my experiences in the realm of nightmares and comic books.

He then explained—somewhat condescendingly—that many beginning therapists suffered from the same type of "confusion" as I did. I wasn't feeling the presence of a mystical "force," I was feeling my inner reaction to how resistant patients were to change. In conclusion, he reminded me what a frustrating process therapy was and that I had to accept this without resorting to fairy tales. Strangely, I left that meeting even more convinced that what I was dealing with was real.

INTRODUCING PART X

Now I had to convince my patients. I had one advantage I didn't have with my supervisor. He accepted nothing without scientific proof. My patients didn't care about proof; they wanted relief—that would be its own proof.

This mysterious force appeared in my patients as doubt and worry, suspiciousness and withdrawal, impulsive desire for drugs and sex—and any other symptom strong enough to cripple their functioning. The variations were endless.

The guy with the gun controlled each of these patients. The specific symptoms—panic, chronic lateness, perfectionism, social avoidance, etc.—are his bullets. His goal isn't to kill you, it's to scare you out of reaching your potential. Something with this kind of power deserved a name. "The guy with the gun" was too awkward and didn't do justice to its mysterious power.

I decided to call it "Part X." It was a fitting name for something off-limits and dangerous—a force whose mysterious power had to be respected. Naming it "Part X" wasn't a coincidence. As a "part" of you, it is intrinsic to your human identity, a *permanent* part of you, just like your heart and brain.

But there was another reason to describe it as a "part" of you. If it was only a part, *there had to be another part.* And this "other" part was the opposite of Part X. Rather than limiting you, it unlocks access to the Life Force. Rather than blocking your growth, it opens your potential. This other part is what most people think of as their soul.

Giving Part X a name made it real in a way it wasn't before. But as excited as I was about my discovery, I didn't know how my patients would react to a new concept presented by an enthusiastic—but very young—psychiatrist. I remember being alone in my office, pacing the floor and rehearsing what I would say to convince them Part X was real and extremely dangerous.

To my surprise, they didn't need convincing. The concept of a universal force lurking behind their symptoms rang true immediately. They liked its name and they liked being able to identify the source of their misery. In a very short time, most of them could identify it in themselves.

I learned something important from this. The average person's mind is a jumbled mess. They have no clarity about where they need to go, nor do they know what's keeping them from getting there. To change, they need to bring order out of this chaos. Intellectual theories about the causes of their situations won't help—*people need constructs that relate to their actual experience.* That's why they accepted Part X so easily; they could *feel* its presence. True faith—in a person, an idea, a decision—isn't based on a logical conclusion you've come to; it's something you feel.

Once Part X had a name and became real in the eyes of my patients, the floodgates of their curiosity opened. If something they'd never heard of before was at the root of their problems, they wanted to know what it was, how it got there, and what to do about it. These were good questions I didn't yet have the answers to.

The biggest challenge was explaining how a single force could create a variety of seemingly unrelated symptoms.

From what I could observe, the most obvious thing my patients' problems had in common was pain. Not the natural pain that's a reaction to death, illness, economic reversal, loss of a friend, and so on. That's *necessary* pain. It's unavoidable and in fact can help you get through the difficult parts of life. Necessary pain serves as a warning that your survival or well-being may be at stake; it keeps you in touch with reality, bringing you to the present so you can see if you need to take action.

What my patients were feeling was *unnecessary* pain. This pain isn't a reaction to anything real; it's proactively generated by Part X, which creates a problem you don't need to have and offers a solution that makes it worse. Far from helping you get through adversity, it makes life harder than it has to be. With unnecessary pain, you're not reacting to the world as it is, you're reacting to the world Part X has created.

This is the key to understanding Part X. It doesn't just sit back and root against you; X is a dynamic force with an agenda it never stops pursuing. Part X is driven to *create unhappiness* the way a great artist is driven to create beauty.

Part X exploits the fact that human beings are complacent. We ignore danger until it's knocking on our door. By the time we become aware of it, the danger has already established a beachhead in our mind. From there, it moves to crush our spirit, limit our future, and doubt the reality of our own potential. The real danger is not being aware of what Part X is doing to you.

It's possible to defeat Part X and take your soul and your future back. But even the most powerful weapon is useless against an enemy you can't see. Step one, therefore, is to rec-ognize *your* personal version of Part X—how it makes itself known in your own life.

THE POWER OF IMPOSSIBILITY

To find something—especially something as devious as Part X—you have to know where to look. Part X is invisible, but it leaves tracks in your inner experience. And the X experience that's most universal is the sense of being stuck—unable to move forward, unable to change, unable to reach some goal that's important to you. When you've hit a wall in life and you have no idea how to get past it, you're walking in the tracks of Part X.

The place you're stuck, the goal that's out of reach, needn't be something with status or power attached to it. What matters is that it's meaningful to you. You may want to be more vulnerable with your partner, but you're afraid of how they'll respond; you may want to start a completely new career, but you don't know how to take the first step; or you may want to overcome your fear of flying, but the thought fills you with dread.

Whatever goal you're pursuing, at some point you'll meet an obstacle. All human endeavors present difficulties and complications. These stumbling blocks are a natural part of life. It's when a single setback expands and intensifies until all ability to grow is shut down that Part X has entered the picture. It's as if you've hit a wall so high you can't see over it. All you can see—written in huge graffiti-style letters—is the word "IMPOSSIBLE." Part X doesn't say, "Quite Diffi-cult" or "A Real Challenge." It's telling you to give up and go home; you've hit a dead end.

X has taken something that is difficult—facing the pain of loneliness, the confusion of entering a business you know nothing about, the humiliation of looking self-conscious in front of an audience—and made it seem impossible and in-surmountable. Part X has performed a kind of dark, destruc-tive magic.

Part X is good at performing its negative alchemy in commonplace situations. Joan was a seventeen-year-old high school student who had intense anxiety when she was away from home. This had been a lifelong problem. Sleepovers, visits to faraway relatives, and school field trips were difficult for her.

She knew her fears weren't rational, but when her panic started it felt impossible to bring it under control. Part X was less interested in the details of her fears than in leaving her with the sense that she couldn't overcome them. X's goal was to contaminate her with the sense of defeat, as if impos-sibility were a poisonous substance.

Joan was an unusually gifted soccer player, but as X spread its psychic poison, traveling with the school team be-came more difficult. She began to lose confidence on the field. Normally an aggressive attacker, she became passive, hang-ing back and avoiding contact.

Part X spread the sense of "it's impossible" beyond the inability to leave home; now it included the inability to com-pete in a sport she'd had tremendous success in. And until it was stopped, X would keep spreading the toxic power of impossibility until all growth was out of reach and all future dreams were destroyed. This expanding sense of impossibility is the secret of Part X's power. It's how it takes an ordinary psychological problem and expands it until you're crippled.

In Joan's case, X was remarkably consistent in its efforts. *Every* time she tried to move out into the world, Part X was right there to remind her to be terrified and paralyzed.

THE POWER OF REPETITION

Part X is persistent in perpetuating the world view it wants you to have—much like a dictator can control an entire population by repeating a lie until it is accepted as the truth. The lie that a dictator uses is that they are the only one who can solve people's problems. Part X also brainwashes us. Its lie is that *nothing* can solve your problem; it's impossible and you should give up trying.

Psychology can play into that lie by focusing too much on the past. This is an invitation for Part X to deepen the sense of impossibility. Imagine that your past is represented by a series of pictures in an exhibition at a museum; each picture represents one event in your life. Part X is the curator, choosing which events get into the show, but X picks only the most negative and painful events. Why? Because when you relive those events, your sense of who you are and what your potential is shrinks.

We want to believe that we assess the world rationally,

when actually Part X dominates our worldview. By repeating negative experiences over and over again, it creates the sense that negativity is all there is. Part X can replay a single negative experience or search your past for a whole variety of them. It can even construct future bad experiences that haven't happened yet. We think of this as worry, which it is, but worry is a tool in Part X's crusade to flood you with negativity.

We all have known someone whose outlook is dominated by Part X. Whether they look backwards and complain about the past or look forward and worry about the future, they radiate negativity and the sense that the world can't accommodate their plans and desires. When you spend too much time with them, you can feel their frustration, cynicism, and discontent rubbing off on you, threatening your own Life Force.

IT'S NOT WHAT YOU THINK, IT'S WHAT YOU DO

Everything you do either expands the sense of what is possible or adds to the feeling that nothing is possible. That extra drink after dinner, fighting with your spouse in front of the kids, those four hours in front of the TV—you know these things aren't good for you, but you continue to do them anyway. Part X has strong-armed you, leaving you with the sense that you can't control yourself, even though you know how destructive your behavior is. Rationality is no match for Part X.

Maybe you want to go back to school, or lose twenty

pounds, or find a spiritual community that inspires you. You're in a test of wills with Part X—although Part X would prefer that you don't know it. X works toward its usual goal—making you helpless and hopeless in a world of impossibility. It's your actions, more than your thoughts, that dictate who wins.

If it can't stop you from taking action it will get you to take the wrong kind of action. One of its most effective strategies—and biggest lies—is to tell you that only large, dramatic actions count. That's the opposite of the truth. *The highest energies enter through the smallest actions.* The importance of small steps is that they can be repeated over and over, creating a nonstop channel for the Life Force.

If you want to go back to school, start with a single class at night and see if that feels like the right choice. If you want to lose twenty pounds, start by skipping dessert at your next meal. If you're looking for a spiritual community, start by asking those around you what works for them. Focusing on huge, symbolic victories—like switching suddenly to a crash diet—will lead you to quit after a few defeats.

No matter how impossible it might feel to change the way you act, there is *always* something you can do to get yourself moving. That's what makes it important to be able to identify Part X as it emerges in *your* life. Recognizing its presence *is* an action, and, when done with discipline, this action becomes the first step in freeing yourself from the prison Part X has you trapped in.

IDENTIFYING YOUR OWN PART X

This short exercise will introduce you to your own Part X as it emerges in your life.

- Remember a specific time in your life when you felt stuck, when you were unable to change something or to reach a desired goal. The goal needn't be dramatic or noteworthy, as long as it was important to you. It can be related to relationships, career, creativity, parenting, or any other part of life. It can be from last week or years ago. If you're having trouble finding something specific, pick a whole area of life that you've always found difficult. The only requirement is that you feel helpless, stopped by something inside you. Notice the place that you get stuck—at that moment Part X has appeared. Feel its presence around you. Say to yourself, "This is Part X."

We call this process "labeling." You're learning to recognize the unique qualities that identify your personal Part X. As simple as it is, it's a crucial building block for everything that will come later.

THE IMPORTANCE OF LABELING

To stop Part X, you have to catch it in the act. That's not as easy as it sounds. Part X sneaks up on you, and does it quickly. This gives it momentum. As Joan, our high school soccer player, listened to Part X's warnings about leaving the house, she lost confidence that she could get her panic under control. The poisonous attitude of "I can't do it, it's impossible" gathered momentum and quickly spread to the rest of her life.

You need to stop X before it gains momentum. Just the way a surgeon has to stop the bleeding in the emergency room in order to see what needs to be done, you need to stop Part X from "bleeding" its negativity into your psyche. If you can't you're left with the crippling sense of "There's nothing I can do about this."

But stopping Part X isn't the same thing as suturing a blood vessel. Part X is without physical form. It's a force and can only be stopped by the infinite energy of the Life Force.

The fact that you can recognize Part X and call out its presence means you are *not* Part X. If you were, you wouldn't be able to do the labeling. So every time you label Part X, you activate the part of you that's free. This part is your soul, the part of you that can choose how you look at the world.

The more you label Part X, the more you activate your soul. This gives you direct access to the Life Force—the driver of your evolution, the source of your hidden potentials—and with it the sense that anything is possible.

When Joan discovered the power of her soul, it was a revelation. She could now see that Part X was behind the fears that were crippling her on and off the soccer field. No longer a passive victim of Part X, for the first time in memory she saw a way out of the world of impossibility.

COMMITMENT TO TAKING ACTION

The factor that separates those who free themselves from Part X from those who don't is consistency. Part X will be relentless in its efforts to crush you with the sense of impossibility. Your commitment to labeling its presence must be just as relentless if you hope to take back control of your own soul. Real commitment means making a promise to do something and then *keeping that promise*—over and over again.

That means doing, not just thinking. You either act or you don't—nothing else matters. There are two kinds of action. The first is *outer action*. It is what it sounds like, things you do in the world around you. We have a clear idea of what most people mean when they use the word *action*. You go to your computer and write your new résumé or you don't. You cancel a meeting to see your kid in the school play or you don't. You confront your boss or you don't.

There's a second kind of action we're much less aware of. It's called *inner action*. Just as outer action is meant to affect the world around you, inner action is meant to affect the world inside you. This is the world of your thoughts and feelings—your inner state. The battle between you and Part X happens in this inner world. It's the battle for your soul.

Part X attacks by flooding your inner world with feelings of failure, negativity, and self-doubt. If you don't fight back, X creates a vision of a bleak future stripped of all sense of possibility.

And most of the time, you don't fight back. Not because you don't want to, but because you don't know how. This is an inner war—bombs and bullets are worthless. You need weapons that work inside you, weapons that can change your inner state.

Our work and our passion is to present you with these inner weapons. But you won't be able to use them if you don't recognize Part X attacking. Labeling is the first line of defense: it identifies the enemy so you can fight back.

In the inner world, commitment is even more crucial than in the outer world. That means making a promise to label Part X and keeping that promise, day after day. It's only the first step, but it reminds you there is a real enemy inside that won't quit in its efforts to crush your spirit.

But no matter how many weapons you have, "killing" Part X is impossible. Like the monster coming back from the grave in the last moments of a horror film, it always returns. That doesn't mean you have to accept its pessimistic view of life. But it does mean that—at any time—you're subject to attack. It requires a kind of spiritual alertness to catch these attacks as soon as they begin. Labeling Part X acts as your early-warning system.

In the more poetic language of the nineteenth century, the crucial importance of labeling Part X is summed up by the famous phrase "Eternal vigilance is the price of liberty."

But to make it work, you need commitment. Commitment doesn't require natural intelligence, athletic ability, successful friends, or a higher degree—it just means you do what you say you're going to do. My basketball career wasn't what you'd call wildly successful, but I learned what it felt like to be committed. Later on, I was able to transfer that ability to other parts of life.

Over thirty years ago, I met my coauthor, Barry Michels,

at a seminar I conducted. When I met him, he'd already had a successful career as a lawyer and was beginning a second one as a therapist. He had an extraordinary (and somewhat annoying) ability to interrogate me about Part X and any other aspect of my work he could get me to talk about.

At first, I wrote it off as the result of his legal training. Because the whole point of what I was doing was a commitment to action—both inner and outer—I was suspicious of someone just gathering information. It took months before I realized how fortunate I was to have met him. He turned out to be one of the most committed people I had ever met.

He shared with me that he ended each session by giving patients "something to do" before he saw them again. I had long felt this involvement of the patient between sessions was the key to creating real change. Most impressively, there was nothing he would ask of his patients that he wouldn't ask of himself. His unflagging commitment to defeating Part X is an inspiration to everyone around him.

Chapter Two

Fighting for the Life Force

Barry learns to identify and defeat Part X and discovers his Life Force—a level of excitement, enthusiasm, and creativity beyond anything he'd imagined.

NOTHING MAKES YOU FEEL QUITE AS INCOMPETENT as sitting face-to-face with your first psychotherapy patient. For me, this took place in a dilapidated social service agency where I interned during my first year of graduate school. Decorated with tattered posters from earlier decades ("Make Love Not War," "Freeze Rents Not Wages"), my office was a small cubicle with a coffee-stained carpet and a molded plastic chair where the patients sat. I sat in a frayed "executive" chair that toppled over if I leaned back too far— I was always on the verge of looking like a complete fool.

In a sense, I was a fool. Every first-timer is. No amount of poring over textbooks, listening to lectures, or taking exams can possibly prepare you for dealing with real people who are in pain and looking to you (often desperately) for solutions. My patients came from all walks of life: many were poor, but, to my surprise, the majority were middle-class people who'd fallen on hard times through no fault of their own. Almost all of them were older and had more life experience than I'd had, cloistered in privileged schools and cushy jobs.

What amazed me the most, however, was how they poured their hearts out to me, vulnerably placing themselves in my hands. I was awed by the courage this took, and more than anything, I wanted to help them in ways that would justify their faith in me.

I failed, again and again, though it wasn't for lack of trying. I had steeped myself in the prevailing methodology of the time, psychodynamic psychotherapy. The theory was that once a patient achieved insight into what caused their problem, their symptoms would go away. One patient complained of constant anxiety and we traced it back to the bleak environment he'd grown up in—his father had had a terminal illness and his mother had been overworked and unavailable. Another patient wanted to stop choosing emotionally unavailable men, and we discovered it had started with a cold, uncaring father whose love she craved but never received.

My patients liked knowing how they got stuck in these habit patterns, but the explanations, by themselves, didn't get them unstuck. Deep down, my doubts about psychodynamic theory began to grow. I kept asking myself, "Why would understanding what *caused* a problem *solve* the problem? Doesn't the patient have to do something different in the here and now?"

I didn't know the answer. But I found myself yearning to give my patients something more than insight into their past—something they could do in the present to start changing their lives. I didn't know it at the time, but I was longing for the revolutionary form of healing I was destined to learn from Phil Stutz.

Fate wasn't ready to introduce us yet, so after my schooling and internship I started my own practice, experimenting with an alternative theory of psychotherapy called cognitive behavioral therapy (CBT). Instead of analyzing the past, a CBT therapist directs patients to change problematic thoughts and behaviors in the present. Here was a theory that made sense to me. When a patient's daughter failed a math exam, I trained him to replace an exaggerated conclusion ("She'll never get into college!") with a more realistic one ("It's normal for kids to struggle, and there are resources that can help her do better next time"). The patient felt less anxious, stopped putting so much pressure on his daughter, and adopted a problem-solving approach with her instead. Gradually, we generalized this approach to all of his catastrophic thoughts.

I even used CBT techniques on myself. Most of my life, I'd been plagued with irrationally harsh self-criticism— a contemptuous voice in my head disparaged everything I did. "You suck as a therapist. You're not a good friend. You'll never amount to much as a person." In keeping with CBT, whenever I heard this voice I would remind myself of all the contrary evidence: "I completed my college requirements in three years and graduated with high honors, my friends seem to like me, and so far most of my patients keep coming back. I must be doing *something* right."

It worked sometimes. But often these reality checks fell flat. To be honest, they often sounded ridiculous, like the goopy self-affirmations of Stuart Smalley on *Saturday Night Live:* "I'm good enough, I'm smart enough, and doggone it, people like me." Worse, sometimes my attempts at self-correction would provoke even more vicious responses from the voice: "Right. You think your patients come back because you're helping them? They come back because they're *desperate*. The only difference between you and a dope dealer is you sell false hope instead of drugs."

It felt like I was dealing with something much more powerful than what CBT called dysfunctional thoughts. The voice was more like a powerful undertow dragging me down into a world in which change was impossible, in which I was and always would be woefully inadequate. In that world, no evidence to the contrary would ever make any difference.

I wasn't the only one who spent time in this painful place; I saw patient after patient fall into it. Their symptoms varied—worry, loneliness, lack of motivation, obsessive anger—but most of them found that changing their thoughts didn't allow them to climb out of the hole they were in.

I had rejected psychodynamic theory because its focus on the past failed to provide patients a way of changing in the present. CBT recognized the need for change in the present, but it underestimated the challenge: its techniques were no match for an inner force that could overwhelm rational thinking and make change seem impossible.

Two theories down the drain, I felt the pressure of what was at stake: I wanted to help my patients, to justify their faith in me. Even more fundamentally, I wanted to have faith in myself. What theory was going to give me that?

DISCOVERING THE LIFE FORCE

I was about to discover the truth: theories don't matter; only the Life Force could give me what I was searching for. But I'd never even heard the term *Life Force*. Even if I had, it wouldn't have been enough: you have to experience it to tap into its benefits. Fortunately, fate decided it was time for me to meet Phil. A friend told me about a psychiatrist who was giving a seminar, adding mysteriously that he was unlike any shrink he'd ever seen. Desperate for solutions, I went.

All my notions of psychotherapy were overturned in the first five minutes of that seminar. It started with Phil himself: his thick New York accent and affinity for blunt street language made him the opposite of most shrinks. I was raised by parents who were active in the psychoanalytic community in Los Angeles, and I'd met quite a few psychiatrists. With some notable exceptions, most were stiff, reserved, and formal. They knew all about *theories* of human behavior, but they held actual human beings at a distance, as if they gave off a bad smell. In contrast, Phil was beyond informal; he made jokes at his own expense and, once he got to know me, made fun of me as well. He had an endless supply of enthusiasm and an infectious, ineradicable belief in everyone's potential; you got the feeling he would say or do *anything* to help you achieve it.

As a person, Phil defied my expectations, but the way he set up the seminar crushed them. As I found my seat in the hotel ballroom, I was expecting a sedate, thoughtful lecture exploring theories of human psychology and how Phil's approach differed from the ones I'd learned in school.

You can imagine my surprise when he started things off by asking each one of us to get up in front of the group and talk about whatever problems we had. I could hear the contemptuous voice beginning to gear up and found myself looking for the nearest exit, wondering if there was a way to slip out unnoticed. As my turn approached, I broke out in a sweat. With no way out, I stood up and described my chronic self-criticism. Before I sat down, I cracked a joke at my own expense: "Right now I'm thinking I sucked at conveying how self-critical I am."

It got a laugh, but Phil wasn't smiling. Looking me straight in the eye, he asked, "Did you enjoy putting yourself down like that?"

I closed my eyes for a moment and became aware of the sadness, the inner sense of betrayal I felt whenever I gave in to the voice. "No. I hate it."

"Good. Don't even think about ever doing that again."

Looking back, that was the moment I stopped *thinking* about change, and started *working* on it. In my adult life, no one had ever ordered me to do anything like Phil had. I wasn't offended; in fact, I was galvanized. Phil's eyes blazed with such determination that, for the first time, I truly believed I could—and must—stop beating myself up. I didn't know *how*, but he'd ignited an urge to fight for myself in a way I never had before.

How had this happened? I had felt Phil's Life Force—his inextinguishable commitment to human potential—and it had sparked my own. As if reading my mind, he launched into a description of the Life Force and how it creates possibility in situations where change seems impossible. It was good to have a name for it, but I was even more fascinated with how it felt inside: I was motivated, determined, willing to risk everything—and it felt like change was possible, right now, in this moment.

A million questions bubbled up inside me. Was this what psychotherapy was supposed to be about—awakening the force of change that lay dormant in every patient? Maybe my instincts had been right—to make a real difference, therapy couldn't be a leisurely stroll into one's past or a superficial exercise in replacing one thought with another. It had to be much more immediate than that: change had to happen *now*, and it had to mobilize the Life Force inside the patient, not retreat to the level of abstract theories.

But how was I going to gain regular access to this mysteriously galvanizing "Life Force"—much less induce it in my patients? I learned that the first step was to identify its enemy—Part X. This was easy for me because it was the voice in my head constantly attacking me. Phil taught us how to label X, and I was determined to start the moment I left the seminar. I was excited. I felt like I'd learned something that could change my life. There was an enemy inside me, and I was determined to catch it in the act of sabotaging me.

PART X IS EVERYWHERE

The days following the seminar were disquieting, to say the least. Now that I was on the lookout for it, I realized Part X was attacking me all the time—so frequently that I missed a lot of opportunities to label it. Phil had warned us this would happen, so I just kept trying and gradually got better at it.

Here are just a few of the ways it attacked me:

I'm listening to an AM radio duo on my way to work— cracking up at a prank phone call they've just made. Part X: "Some people listen to NPR or mind-improving audiobooks on their morning commute; you waste your time on this garbage."

My wife, busy with a million things, hands our daughter to me for a moment. She starts wriggling out of my arms, eventually screaming and crying for her mother. Part X: "See? Even a child can tell how inept you are as a father!"

I'm at a loud party where I don't know anybody. It seems like everyone has someone to talk to except me. I feel shy about striking up a conversation with a total stranger. With every passing minute, Part X is making me feel more like some sort of aberrant freak: "There's something very wrong with you—people sense it; that's why nobody wants to talk to you."

What astonished me was how deft Part X was at taking these innocuous situations and turning them against me.

And I wasn't the only one. As my patients learned to label Part X, they noticed it doing the same to them. Part X spoiled one patient's day at the beach by flooding her with fears of a shark attack. An innocent comment about another patient's weight triggered a Part X–induced shame spiral. Another patient received a minor rebuke at work, and Part X provoked a job-ending confrontation with his boss. Part X was so dexterous at turning every situation against people I began to describe it to my patients as "an equal opportunity mindfuck."

At first, many patients feel overwhelmed trying to spot Part X all day, especially when they're not used to it. Don't get stressed about this. You're going to miss a lot of X attacks in the beginning. But stick with it, no matter how many times you fail. In a short time, you'll get good at it and begin to see some amazing results.

SEEING IS FREEING

I noticed a change within the first week. I began to feel lighter and freer. Simply catching X in the act—over and over again—helped me gain a sense of distance from it. It was like plucking an invisible parasite from inside me and pushing it out in front where I could see it. Just calling it out created a buffer zone between it and me—a separation that gave me a choice over whether or not to listen to it. I still made the wrong choice often, but just knowing I *had* a choice made X less overwhelming.

But there were even more important rewards to come. Traditional psychotherapy, by focusing on your past, unwittingly encourages you to *live* in the past. Labeling Part X, which takes place in the present, allows you to *let go* of the past.

I'm a good example. The roots of my chronic self-criticism had been obvious to me long before I met Phil. My mother was a desperately unhappy person. When I was a kid, she made it seem like I was the only person in her life who could make her happy. To put it in her words, "Barry, if it weren't for you, I'd kill myself." I now know that was her Part X talking, but as a kid I felt responsible for her and did everything I could to help her feel better—empathizing with her, encouraging her, making her laugh, etc. It often worked in the moment, but eventually she'd slip back into the same state—depressed and enraged because (in her mind) everyone had let her down.

Gradually, I began to get down on myself, feeling like I'd failed her. The more independent I became, the more she agreed, turning her rage on me and confirming my sense of failure. Obviously, this was where my pervasive self-criticism came from.

My problem with conventional psychology was that I already understood all of this, and the insight didn't help. If anything, going over it again and again seemed to play right into Part X's hands. It was one thing to trace the problem back to my mother, but Part X wanted more: it wanted me to keep *blaming* her for it. If Part X could keep me focused on what my mother did to me in the past, it could hide what it was doing to me in the present: keeping the self-loathing alive. I knew guys who'd been psychoanalyzed and who— well into their sixties and seventies—still blamed their parents for everything wrong in their lives. I was horrified at the prospect of becoming one of these perpetual "victims." I wanted to stop all of it—blaming myself as well as her.

I felt so strongly about this I decided to label Part X not only when the inner voice was putting me down, but also whenever it tried to shift the blame to my mother: "No wonder you're so self-critical—your mother demanded too much of you, she was too hard on you," etc. I began to see that this was Part X, blaming her for starting what *it* was perpetuating. Over time, this helped me accept, once and for all, that my real enemy wasn't my mother—it was Part X.

This was not only more effective than going over the past, it was also fairer to her. The truth was, my mother was a great parent in a lot of ways. She was imaginative and always encouraging of my creative pursuits. She instilled in me a deep sense of fairness and empathy for the underdog, and she gave me the courage to face a myriad of childhood fears. X wanted me to forget all of these gifts and focus only on what she'd done to victimize me. The more I saw X as the real enemy, the more balanced my view of her became: she got some things right and some things wrong, but it was now my responsibility to take over the job of shaping who I was. I liked that Phil's approach made me, not her, responsible for my own evolution.

As a newly minted psychotherapist, I began to realize that this was a weakness of traditional psychology. By focusing exclusively on the past, it unwittingly reinforces Part X's mission to hold you back. Both are telling you that your past is determinative of who you are in the present. This ignores the most powerful weapon you have as a human being: *the will to change your thoughts, feelings, and behavior right now, in the present.* Traditional therapy often falls prey to Part X, keeping you stuck in the childlike stance of blaming your past. Labeling Part X elevates you into emotional adulthood; you're aware of how the past affected you, but determined to take responsibility for who you are in the present.

As Phil had predicted in the seminar, consistently calling out Part X did something else for me. It activated my "soul," the avatar of creative forces. I'd always harbored a secret ambition to write, but with Part X telling me I'd just embarrass myself, I never had the nerve to try. Now, with some breathing room from the doom-whisperer, I found myself jotting down ideas when they came to me. Eventually, those notes blossomed into an essay about my relationship with my father. It took months, but when I was finished I was proud of the result. So proud, in fact, I made a beginner's mistake: I forgot about Part X.

EVERYONE BACKSLIDES

Despite your best intentions, you'll do this too. At some point, you'll start to gain a feeling of mastery over Part X. Your symptoms will lessen or disappear completely, and in the flush of victory, the practice of identifying X will slip away. You'll forget about Part X . . . but it won't forget about you. As you let down your guard, it will gradually reassert itself.

In the weeks after I finished the essay about my father, I sank back into the mire of self-hatred. At first it was about the essay. ("It's sappy and confessional and guess what—

nobody cares about you or your relationship with your father.") But quickly it mushroomed into an indictment of everything. ("When you die, nothing you've done will have made any difference to anybody. Your entire existence is a joke.")

These attacks are hard to fight, because by forgetting about Part X you're unprepared for them. At first I couldn't find my bearings. I found myself in a bottomless pit of self-loathing and despair. But I had one advantage I'd never had before. I knew about Part X and had already identified it thousands of times. That gave me the presence of mind to take a deep breath and collect myself. "This is Part X," I said to myself. "You're in its world now, but don't lose yourself." It was a very dark place, but by constantly differentiating myself from Part X, I'd found a small, inextinguishable light inside of me—the light of my own soul, separate from X.

THE LIGHT BURIED IN THE DARKNESS

I visualized this hellhole I'd fallen into: a blasted, barren wasteland without hope, prospects, or possibilities. In my mind's eye, I saw Part X—the iron-fisted overlord of this dark realm. With a sense of revulsion, I realized I'd allowed X to drag me down here my entire life, releasing me only after my spirit was drained. I had never escaped of my own free will. I felt a flash of anger—partly at my own passivity, but mostly at Part X. Then, out of nowhere, I felt something new: defiance. I had the desire to fight back. I heard my own words resounding through my soul: "I won't let you turn me against myself anymore." My inner voice was as vehement as Phil's when he'd ordered me to stop attacking myself.

I had no idea where this boldness came from, but suddenly I felt stronger than I ever had before—a tough, disciplined warrior willing to fight for the rest of his life if need be. Part X had vanished into thin air.

After I calmed down, I retraced my steps from the beginning. Taking a creative risk (by writing the essay) had been like thumbing my nose at Part X. It was losing its grip over me, so it hit back, subtly at first, then with a crescendo of self-loathing. I had forgotten about Part X, so initially I succumbed. But it was temporary. I suddenly remembered I could separate myself from X and see it for what it was: a vicious enemy bent on diminishing me whenever it could.

At that moment, something entirely new emerged: my own Life Force. This was the most unexpected thing of all. I felt it as a kind of bold defiance—the way you'd feel standing up to a bully. In you, it might show up in a completely different form, like an enhanced sense of purpose, clarity, the ability to express yourself or solve problems. Whatever form it shows up in, it will give you powers you didn't know you had. With these powers comes a sense that everything is possible.

The Life Force was what enabled me to overcome Part X. I now knew that this was what I'd been searching for from the beginning. It was the yearning I'd felt as an intern, wanting to answer my patients' pleas with something more than insight into their past. It was the vehemence with which Phil had challenged whatever stood in the way of people's potential. It was the excited determination with which I left Phil's seminar and started labeling X as if my life depended on it. The Life Force gave me the courage and the creativity to write about my father, and it lifted me out of the hole X put me in after I finished the essay.

The Life Force also forever changed the way I conducted myself as a therapist. My patients didn't know how to put it in words, but every single one of them was asking me to embody more Life Force—to convey to them that change was possible and that I could show them the way. I had always thought my best sessions were the ones where I explained things clearly. It turned out my patients liked the ones where I was *passionate about change.* It mattered less to them what I said than what they sensed stirring in my soul. I stopped trying to emulate the detached, cerebral style of the shrinks I'd grown up with. Instead, I found myself acting more like the coaches of my kids' sports teams. They wanted every player to throw themselves fully into every play—to stretch beyond where they'd ever gone before. I wanted to inspire that same all-out intensity in my patients. It was what had enabled me to climb out of the hole X had put me in—and I knew it would do the same for them.

THE TOOLS: PORTALS TO LIFE

The Life Force is the opposite of Part X. If X is the prophet of impossibility, the Life Force is the herald of limitless potential, creating the sense that everything can change right now, in the present. It knows, better than you do, what you're capable of—and it gives you the energy to become the highest version of yourself. I've never met anyone who couldn't benefit from more of it.

So how can you gain more access to it?

As strange as it sounds, Part X leads you to it. Think about what happened to me. If Part X hadn't dragged me down into its hellhole, I wouldn't have found the determination to fight my way back up again. By working as hard as it did to destroy my Life Force, Part X unwittingly pointed the way to it. In my case, I was lucky—all it took was labeling X over and over again for me to find the power to fight back. But as you'll discover, most of the time just labeling X isn't enough. You'll need a consistent, reliable way to tap into the Life Force when Part X is attacking you. That's why you need tools.

Which tool you use will depend on how Part X is attacking you. In the coming chapters, we'll identify the four basic lines of attack Part X uses with almost everybody. These are X's most effective strategies; we've never met anyone who doesn't fall prey to at least one of them, and most people suffer from all four. Each creates a different type of deadness—in which X has drained the spirit, vitality, and sense of meaning that is your birthright.

Here's the best way to picture what Part X is trying to accomplish with these strategies: imagine that life is a difficult climb up a mountain path. You get closer to fulfilling your potential with every step you take, but Part X is constantly working to stop your progress. As often as it can, it shoves you into a hole; you stop ascending. The pit I fell into involved feelings of constant inadequacy. Yours might be chronic worry, procrastination, or moodiness. Whatever hole

X puts you in, it consists of a set of thoughts, feelings, and behaviors that drain you until it seems impossible to climb out. That's the key to Part X's success: it not only shoves you into the hole, it gets you to *stay* there, languishing. If it succeeds, you eventually forget you're even in a hole. You begin to believe that what you're experiencing is all there is to life.

Here are the four most common pitfalls:

1. **SELF-GRATIFICATION:** Part X gets you to give in to impulses like using alcohol or drugs, overeating, surfing the Internet, checking social media, texting, staying up too late, shopping, gambling, playing videogames, watching TV, etc. It doesn't care which impulse you give in to, or even if it's the same impulse each time. Its long-term goal is much more treacherous: it wants you to become addicted to immediate gratification. When that happens, you won't be able to tolerate the inevitable delays, setbacks, and frustrations you'll have to face to achieve anything. You'll make the classic bargain with the devil and throw away your long-term potential in exchange for a series of meaningless, short-term indulgences.

2. **LETHARGY:** Part X convinces you that you don't have enough energy to meet the demands of life and gets you to slack off on things you need to do for yourself and the people around you. It's time to exercise, but you can't get up from the couch, where you're mesmerized by the TV. You're too tired to corral your kids into bed, so you allow them to stay up later than they should. There's an important phone call you have to return, but you keep postponing it because you know it's going to be draining. If you continually withdraw

from life's demands, tasks are left undone, you lose touch with people, and opportunities pass you by. Life moves on without you.

3. **DEMORALIZATION**: Part X wants to convert normal discouragement into hopelessness so you'll quit trying and give up on the things that are most important to you. A woman searches for a loving partner, but after multiple setbacks stops dating altogether. A teenage boy works out all summer to make the football team, but gets cut and gives up on sports entirely. An aspiring writer has a novel rejected by four publishers, and can't bring herself to submit anywhere else. Being disappointed from time to time is normal, but if X can get you to feel demoralized, then, like these people, you will quit and give up on yourself and your future.

4. **HURT FEELINGS**: When your feelings get hurt, Part X convinces you not to let go and move on. Your spouse says something snarky and you find yourself fuming about it for hours. A teenager's friends play a practical joke on him and he sulks, refusing to have anything to do with them. A job you wanted goes to a rival despite the fact that you're more qualified; you go on strike, refusing to work as hard as you should. Life is filled with unexpected injuries. If you can't get past the hurt feelings, Part X sabotages you; you stop challenging yourself in new and exciting ways. Your life gets mired in self-pity and self-righteousness.

You've probably fallen into one—or all—of these holes. We all have. There's no shame in that. The real problem is what we do once we fall down: we stay down. That's exactly what Part X wants us to do. The solution is to climb out. As the ancient Chinese philosopher Confucius said, "Our greatest glory is not in never falling, but in rising every time we fall."

By now you understand what *won't* help you rise up: blaming yourself, your past, or the circumstances that put you in the hole. Rising up requires one thing alone: tools. We've created a tool to help you out of each one of these holes. The more frequently you use the tools, the more confident you'll be that you can recover from every Part X attack and continue ascending to your highest potential.

WHAT THE TOOLS GIVE YOU

I have used each of these tools countless times, and I have taught them to innumerable patients. I can attest to their effectiveness. They give you access to the Life Force at the very moment you need it.

At first, when you use the tools, you'll simply be relieved that you can break old habit patterns that have held you back for as long as you remember. You've had weight problems for most of your life, and suddenly you're able to stick to a diet and exercise program. There's a project you've wanted to pursue but you've always been too tired at the end of your workday; now you have the energy to tackle it. There's someone in your life who criticizes everything you do—it's always discouraged you; now it no longer stops you—you're free of the need for their approval.

But solving your immediate problem is just the beginning. If you continue to use the tools, you'll start to notice much broader changes that go beyond the specific problem you were working on. In my case, I felt happier and more motivated. With more energy came greater patience at dealing with the stresses of everyday life—tantrumming kids, disagreements with my wife, anxieties about money, etc. On a more subtle level, my sense of what was possible expanded exponentially. My practice grew and I felt inspired to write essays and books. Eventually Phil and I began to collaborate on various projects. It was like my whole life opened up, and for the first time I actually felt like a success instead of a failure. In sum, I experienced a kind of renaissance.

Don't worry if this much change seems impossible right now. A low Life Force is insidious, affecting every aspect of your life and eroding your sense of what's possible. It's hard to believe, but Part X has trained most people to expect very little of themselves and their lives. You become habituated to a life half-lived, in which you and those around you are uninspired. But no matter what your specific problem is, as you use the tools, your Life Force will expand, and with it your sense of what's possible. Not only will you overcome your specific problem, but *all* obstacles will be easier to overcome. You will begin to experience life as it truly is—limitless.

I am confident of this not because I read it in a book, or because an expert taught it to me, but because I experienced it for myself. I didn't think about it—I *lived* it. I used the tools assiduously, my Life Force increased, and my life got better in every way. That means it won't be enough for you to read about the tools—you'll have to use them. But if you do, your life will change.

THE LIFE FORCE GROWS IN CYCLES

The tools are not magical—they won't eliminate Part X or stop it from pushing you into holes on your way up the mountain. Everyone who's ever worked with the tools—myself included—has had to *continue* using them. There is never a permanent victory, because Part X is always there, fighting against whatever progress you've made.

Some self-help gurus like to paint a rosy picture of how easy it is to change. They don't want to tell you the truth—that no matter how high you climb, you will still find yourself falling into a hole. They're appealing to the lazy, childish part of you that wants X to go away—so you can stop having to use tools against it. We'd rather you know the whole truth—not just the rosy part of it. If you know you're going to fall, you won't get mired in the details of how it happened; instead, you'll see it for what it is—an opportunity to rise back up again as quickly as possible.

When we explain this to our patients, they often object: "Is that all there is to life, falling into holes and climbing out of them again? It seems pointless." It's a question that stretches back into the ages. The ancient Greeks posed the very same question in the myth of Sisyphus, a king whom the gods condemned to roll an immense boulder up a hill, only to watch it roll back down again. He had to repeat this action for eternity. In modern times, his name has become synonymous with useless effort, and his story is interpreted as a metaphor for the meaninglessness of life—a laborious and unending series of futile tasks.

We disagree. Just because a struggle is endless—as the

struggle against Part X is—doesn't make it futile or meaning-less. Most of us look only at what's happening outwardly to Sisyphus—he's engaged in a repetitive effort that yields the same outcome each time. But inwardly something very mean-ingful is happening: his strength, stamina, determination—in short, his Life Force—is growing with every cycle. Sisyphus must roll the rock up in order to get strong, and the gods must roll it back down again for him to get even stronger. Without the downward movement, the inner forces of his personality would stagnate.

This cycle—of going down and fighting your way back up again—is built into the life of every individual. Part X, the enemy of life, drags you down, and your Life Force increases every time you use the tools to rise back up again. This makes Part X an unwitting ally in the expansion of your potential. By trying to limit you, it challenges you to grow even more. If you examine my story—and those in the following chapters—you'll see that's exactly what happened. Part X pushed us down, and we bounced back with even more life energy.

WHAT MAKES LIFE WORTH LIVING

I've been fighting Part X for thirty years now. I am an expert at going down and climbing back up again—and help-ing my patients traverse the same territory in their lives. My Life Force is higher than it's ever been before. I am in a unique position to describe how that improved my life—and how it will expand yours. I've already alluded to some of the changes I experienced: more energy and enthusiasm, more productiv-

ity with less stress, and an enlarged sense of possibility overall in my life.

But there were more profound changes—mysterious and
unexpected. The Life Force changed the entire shape of my
life, affecting how I saw myself and the world. It's difficult to
put these new experiences into words, but they penetrated to
the core of my being. They had to do with three parts of life
that everyone grapples with from childhood on: truth, beauty,
and goodness. These may seem like empty words to you—
they originally did to me. But when my Life Force increased,
they assumed much greater significance. They became life's
highest and holiest ideals—worth living and dying for.

TRUTH. You probably think you don't lie to yourself, but
you do. We all do—constantly. We make resolutions we don't
keep: "I'm going to spend more time with my kids," "I'm
going to lose weight," "I'm going to initiate more intimacy
with my spouse." We blame how stuck we are on our circumstances when really it's our willpower that's lacking. When
there's conflict, we focus on what the other person said or
did, failing to take responsibility for our part in provoking it
or making it worse.

Part X loves these lies—the more the better. Each lie is a
strand in a web of deceit Part X weaves around you, binding
your life and destroying the sense that things can be different.

But as your Life Force increases, something new enters
your life: the strength to see through your own lies. I'm a
good example. The stronger I got, the more my perspective
shifted, and for the first time I saw that constantly criticizing
myself was actually convenient and selfish. It gave me the

perfect excuse to be obsessed with myself. I began to realize that while I was being so hard on myself, the people closest to me were experiencing me as self-absorbed and withdrawn.

It isn't easy to face truths about yourself, but it is liberating. Instead of being stuck in an old script, you're free to write a new one and become the person you've always yearned to be. You'll find yourself living a simpler, more honest, and more direct life—a life of integrity.

BEAUTY. Facing truths about myself and others was only the beginning. I also started to see the whole world differently—alive in a way it had never been before. Suddenly, everything and everyone around me seemed to radiate with a kind of inner grace. The immensity of the sky made me feel part of something much greater than myself; the sparkling eyes of a stranger suddenly moved me to connect with him; a song I'd heard a million times now, for some reason, pierced my heart. Before, I'd experienced everything through a filter that had rendered the world dull and ordinary. Now, with the filter gone, everything seemed extraordinary, vibrating with vitality.

To a much greater degree than you realize, Part X has programmed you to see life as drab and colorless, an endless trek through a meaningless series of obstacles. Part X's world is devoid of beauty and its power to inspire. But as your Life Force gets stronger, you begin to see beauty *everywhere*—a living, breathing spirit and an ever-present source of inspiration. Even things you've judged as ugly—the neon lights along a trash-strewn street, a boarded-up storefront—now seem lit up from within, part of a wondrous creation. The Life Force *inside* has allowed you to perceive the Life Force *outside,* and you realize that it is interwoven throughout all of reality.

GOODNESS. When the outside world bombards you with beauty, it creates a sense of abundance inside. It's like being infused with inspiring energy every moment of the day. I felt so expansive—so filled with everything I'd ever needed— that I found myself wanting to live a more moral life. It sounds trite, but I wanted to be a better person—to not act selfishly or think in small or petty ways. And the hard truths I was facing about myself gave me a specific way to do that.

When you have the courage to face the truth everyone wants to deny—that you have an evil Part X that damages you and the people around you—and when you rise above it by using tools, you become truly virtuous. I began to strive, harder than I ever had before, to live up to the standards I prized the most: courage, patience, and most of all, generosity of spirit. It was as if a new kind of goodness was being born inside me.

CLIMBING TO THE TOP OF THE MOUNTAIN

Truth, beauty, and *goodness* were terms I was familiar with. These were the eternal, unchanging principles that organized the universe; ancient philosophers had dubbed them "transcendentals." I'd studied them my freshman year of college, but at seventeen they meant nothing to me; the only thing I wanted to transcend was my ineptitude with girls.

It wouldn't have mattered even if I had cared. In academia, truth, beauty, and goodness are presented as dry, philosophical concepts, not as real forces that can change who you are. The more I used tools and increased my Life Force, the more real these forces became. They began to give me something I'd never had before: a sense that I was living for something greater than myself. These *ideas* had become *ideals*—I wanted to align myself with them as closely as I could.

Truth, beauty, and goodness are there for everyone to experience. You've had hints of their existence—everyone has. But we want you to experience their presence in a more constant way. All that's required is that you increase your Life Force by going through as many cycles as you can. Every time Part X drags you down and you use tools to bring yourself back up again, you complete a cycle and your Life Force grows. Eventually, your entire being ascends into a realm where truth, beauty, and goodness become forces that make you fully alive. You know why you were born, and your sense of purpose is undeniable. Your soul has found its true place in the universe.

Thirty years ago, I started using the tools in order to solve my problems. I still use them for that reason. But now there's an even stronger reason to use them: they keep me connected to the forces of truth, beauty, and goodness— allowing them to flow through me to those around me.

You now have everything you need in order to learn the tools and start using them. You know who your enemy is and you are familiar with its tactics. You know how to identify it in real time. Most important, you know what's at stake and what's possible. The tools that follow are the weapons that have allowed many others to fight Part X successfully and ascend to their highest potential. They will help you reach yours too.

This is it. There are no excuses; no reasons to delay. It doesn't matter how rich or poor you are, how put together or how screwed up, how good or how bad you think your life is. If you use these tools, *you will get stronger.*

You are ready to climb the mountain—and we're honored to help you on your way to the top.

A User's Guide to the Tools

WHAT ARE TOOLS? TOOLS ARE PRACTICES, SIMPLE techniques that bridge the gap between insight and action. Using them over time enables you to fulfill your potential. You use a tool whenever you find yourself stuck; if you use it *every* time you're stuck, you unlock your potential. Tools help you to cross the threshold and become the person you sensed you could be.

Most likely you're already using some form of tools in your life. Some people use meditation or chanting to induce a relaxed and clear state of mind. Others use visualizations to increase their chances of achieving what they want in life. One difference between these techniques and the tools you're about to learn is that the tools we teach are very quick—they take less than ten seconds to use. This is important, because, unlike meditation and visualization, you'll be using them at the very moment you're experiencing a problem: a delicious dessert is beckoning and you have to resist; your boss rejected your pet project and you have to get over it and come up with something new; your teenager freaks out on you and you want to de-escalate the situation, etc.

We'll walk you through each tool step-by-step. We'll also provide you with "cues" that tell you when to use each tool—situations in life where you typically give in to Part X. One piece of advice before you get started: When our patients learn a tool for the first time, they often worry they're not using it correctly. They have a picture in their minds of how it's "supposed" to feel, and when it doesn't, they give up. Please do not overthink the process of learning the tools. Just read the tool over a few times, then try to use it as often as you can. If you want to make it even easier on yourself, record the tools on an electronic device so you can practice them without having to read the words.

Learning to use tools requires *doing*, not *thinking*. Don't analyze whether you've gotten them right or even if they're working. It might not feel like they're doing anything at first. If you simply use them—again and again—they'll connect you to your Life Force and expand your world in ways you never thought possible.

Chapter Three

The Tool: The Black Sun

Barry explains how the Black Sun can help you resist impulses such as overeating, using alcohol or drugs, surfing the Internet, checking social media, staying up too late, buying things you don't need, calling or texting exes, and more.

Y OU NEVER REALLY KNOW WHAT NEW PATIENTS will be like until the introductions are over. When Susan and Marty walked into my office for their first session, they struck me as a respectful and polite couple, genuinely interested in helping their sixteen-year-old daughter, Ashley, who was spending too much money on clothes. It sounded like an easy case—I could show them how to set limits with her in a few sessions. But within the first five minutes, I realized the problem was much worse than I'd thought—it was like being in a cage with wild animals.

Susan started the ball rolling. She looked at her husband and said, "I promised Ashley I wouldn't tell what she did."

Marty, his voice rising, responded, "Oh, that's just great!

We're here to get guidance from the doctor and you won't even tell him what the problem is." Turning to me, he added, "See, Doc, this is what always happens. I want to *solve* the problems in my family and she just wants to *hide* them."

In a much harsher tone, Susan shot back, "*Solve* problems? You *are* the problem. Why do you think I had to promise Ashley not to tell you she stole money from my purse?"

The veins in Marty's forehead bulged red. "What the . . . !" he sputtered. "Our daughter turns into a criminal and you keep it a secret from me? THIS IS WHY OUR WHOLE HOUSE IS OUT OF CONTROL!"

"I rest my case." Susan smiled serenely. "You're the one who's out of control, and your temper's only the beginning. You think I don't know where you're going when you leave the house at eleven o'clock on a school night? You sure aren't burning the midnight oil at work!" Susan turned to me, her face contorted with disgust. "He says he doesn't want any secrets, but he's at the card clubs every night, gambling away our life savings."

She sat back in her chair triumphantly. Marty was silenced, but it was the silence of a coiled snake. A moment later, he struck back: "And what are you doing at eleven o'clock? Dragging a tub of ice cream out of the freezer! It's revolting. I only started gambling so I wouldn't have to watch you stuff your face every night."

Susan and Marty had put on quite an exhibition, all before I had a chance to open my mouth. In one sense, the fireworks were helpful; they demonstrated that the problem went way beyond Ashley. No one in the family knew how to control themselves. Susan couldn't control herself with food.

Marty gambled and had a hair-trigger temper. Ashley was a shopaholic and a budding thief. There was one more member of the family: Chad, a fourteen-year-old. I hoped he was in better shape than the rest of the family.

Now, with all their problems on the table, Marty and Susan looked at me, each expecting me to side with them. I disappointed both of them. "You guys fight this way all the time, don't you? You know how I know that?" They both looked at the floor. "Neither one of you has any self-control. Gambling, overeating, constantly blaming each other. Why would your daughter control her spending when every day she sees both of you giving in to your worst impulses?"

Marty looked suspicious. "Are you saying Ashley's problem is our fault?"

"No. You can be the best parent in the world and your kids are still going to do dumb things. But if you can't restrain yourself, how are you going to teach Ashley to restrain herself?"

This didn't go over well. Marty was stone-faced as Susan started to cry. Marty made a few attempts to defend his gambling ("It isn't *every* night," "It's the only escape I ever get from this dysfunctional family"), but quickly realized I wasn't buying it. At the end of the session, Susan turned to her husband and said, "No one's ever been this blunt with us before. I think we should come back next week, Marty ... like we said we would." But I could see he was just counting the minutes before he could get out of my office.

After they shuffled out, I sat for a while, my heart pounding. The whole session had felt out of control—like trying to corral a class of preschoolers with a collective sugar rush.

Instead of working constructively to find solutions, Marty and Susan had gotten off on the thrill of hurting each other. They'd come to the session asking for help, but something inside them was rejecting the very help they'd asked for.

This kind of therapy session—unruly, hostile, and unproductive—was a sure sign that Part X had invaded my office. The fighting between Marty and Susan was only the tip of the iceberg. Part X had completely taken over their lives, seducing them (and their daughter) with the lure of immediate gratification. Marty went for fast action, Susan for fast food, and Ashley for fast cash.

THE PROBLEM: IMPULSES

Almost everyone in our society experiences some kind of impulse they can't control. You might compulsively update your Facebook page, buy stuff you don't need, flip people off in traffic, or have "just one more" drink even though you're past your limit. When I hear my phone ping to announce an incoming email or text, I feel like one of Pavlov's dogs— I have to fight the urge to check it, even if I'm involved in something that requires all my attention.

We all have excuses for giving in to these impulses. "It's just a momentary interruption." "I deserve a reward." "To-morrow I'm *definitely* going to turn over a new leaf." But by giving in to these excuses, you're actually participating in your own destruction.

"Destruction" might sound harsh. A single lapse by itself—a dessert that's not on your diet, a purchase over your limit, watching YouTube videos when you should be working—isn't going to ruin your life. But that's what's so devious about Part X. By getting you to give in to one "harmless" urge after another, Part X is creating something much more dangerous: *a self-indulgent way of life*.

THE PRICE OF SELF-INDULGENCE

There's a tremendous cost for this lifestyle: it destroys your future. Whatever you want to create in the future requires that you delay gratification in the present. Let's say your dream is to get a job promotion. To make that happen, there are a lot of steps you might want to take, like cultivating relationships with higher-ups who can help you, taking evening classes to learn the skills you'll need, or putting in extra time on current projects so you can sell yourself when the time comes. Every step of the way, you're likely to be tempted to go out drinking with friends, watch your favorite TV show, or go shopping. But it's only by resisting those impulses that you have a chance of achieving your dream.

This is true no matter what you want to create. The writer who spends hours mindlessly surfing the net has no time or inspiration left to write. The husband who compulsively looks at pornography loses interest in an intimate relationship with his wife. Family members who stay glued to their phones during dinner lose their ability to interact meaningfully with one another.

Self-indulgence exhausts the energy you need in order to get what you want out of life. What's so devious about Part X's strategy is that it drains you drip by drip—so gradually you're not even aware of it. Historically, this process was

seen as the work of the devil in his role as "tempter." He seduces you with small pleasures, each inconsequential in itself.
He waits patiently as you give in time and time again. Little
by little, you lose the willpower to resist his enticements. Finally, you pay the ultimate price: it's too late to accomplish
what you wanted to in life.

Marty and Susan's relationship was a good example of
this process in action. Their inability to resist one-upping
each other with poisoned zingers deprived them of the ability
to discuss, much less solve, their daughter's spending problem.

Fortunately, they received a wake-up call about a month
after our session, in the form of their son's report card. Chad
was a tenth grader and a straight-A student, but in the past
few months he'd been letting his studies slide, wasting all his
time playing videogames. Now he'd come home with Cs and Ds.

This was like dropping a bomb on the family, especially
for Marty. When Marty began his career as a stockbroker,
he'd had high hopes of becoming a "heavy hitter." This never
panned out, partly because he alienated so many people with
his temper. The moment he realized how bright and ambitious Chad was, Marty set about grooming him for success,
delivering nightly harangues on the importance of self-
discipline. Now he saw his son veering off the path to a golden
future and was determined to prevent it. But Chad no longer
seemed to be listening.

It was a measure of his desperation that Marty swallowed
his pride and contacted me. My gut told me that if Susan and
Marty came back together, it would turn into another free-
for-all, so I recommended to both of them that Marty come

in weekly by himself. I've often found that if I can train one person in the family to exercise self-control, the whole family becomes more open to it.

Marty was certainly motivated. "Doc, I know I blew my career, but I can't stand seeing him do the same thing. He's at the point where grades really start to matter for college." He leaned in, his tone urgent, almost pleading. "We've got to turn this around right now, before his end-of-the-year report card ruins his future."

"There's the problem right there," I said.

He looked confused.

"That urgent need to solve Chad's problem *right now!*"

He still looked confused.

"Let me break it down for you. Chad's first impulse when he comes home from school is to escape into a virtual world. You want him to control that impulse and get his work done. That means he has to tolerate frustration, right?"

Marty nodded.

"How would you rate yourself on frustration tolerance? Be honest. When you go home tonight and find out Chad played videogames instead of doing his homework, are you going restrain yourself? No. You're going to freak out and scream at him. Why would he listen to you? You're demanding he do something you don't do yourself. For that matter, why would anyone in the family listen to you?"

Marty looked stricken. This was the first time he realized the price everyone paid for his lack of self-control. With no leader, no structure, and no sense of the future, his family was like a driverless bus, careening out of control; his children had no one to look up to as a role model. Marty, far from being a "problem-solver," was just another infant screaming from the back of the bus—in fact, he was the loudest one. Susan wasn't any better than her husband; her solution to her daughter's theft was to hide it and then soothe her own anxiety with food. She was as out of control as everyone else in the family.

At first it might seem shocking that Marty and Susan went on like this despite the heavy price the family paid. But you've seen people pay an even greater price. Nearly every week brings some new revelation of a politician, sports figure, business leader, or clergyman—holders of the most respected, coveted positions in our culture—crash and burn because they can't control their urges. No matter how many times we witness this, it's impossible not to wonder what they were thinking. How could they not realize they were putting their entire future at risk?

The answer is simple: they were in an altered state. A hallmark of normal consciousness is that you anticipate the consequences of your actions. To do that, you must simultaneously be aware of what you're doing now and what effect it might have on your future. "I'm in a hurry, but if I run out into the street I might get hit by a car."

But what if Part X makes you crave something so intensely that getting it becomes your sole focus? At that moment, your impulses become so strong they blot out all awareness of future consequences.

A junkie is an extreme example of this. When he needs his fix, he'll risk his entire future to get it: fail to show up for work, neglect his children, steal from his parents. The consequences of his actions have no reality for him. You're probably telling yourself, "I'm not a junkie. I would never sink that low." Let's hope that's true, but we all share something in common with the junkie: our cravings put us in an altered state that blinds us to the consequences of our actions.

To get yourself out of this altered state, you have to know when you're in it. We want to teach you how to identify it right now. This exercise will help you.

- Choose an impulse you usually give in to. It might be eating sweets, answering a text while driving, hitting the snooze button on your alarm, buying unnecessary stuff on the Internet, calling an ex-boyfriend when you're lonely, or anything else that comes to mind. Just pick one for now.
- Feel how much you want the thing you chose.
- Make the desire for it even more intense, like you must have it, you can't do without it.
- Eventually, your entire being is filled with an insatiable hunger; it's so intense that nothing else exists.

You've just felt how Part X can create an impulse so strong it blinds you to the consequences of your actions. And in real life (as opposed to an exercise), Part X floods you with these impulses so quickly and with so much force you don't even realize that you're now in an altered state.

But even if you were aware, that alone wouldn't be enough. You have to actively restrain yourself. And you have to do it at the moment you feel the urge. Marty would have to shut up every time he felt like screaming at someone. Susan would have to walk away from the freezer when she felt like digging into the ice cream. Ashley would have to keep her hands to herself whenever she felt like filching money. And when a videogame beckoned, Chad would have to turn away and do his homework.

THE LIE THAT KEEPS US SELF-INDULGENT

Unfortunately, this kind of self-control is rare. We've moved from a culture of self-sacrifice and self-discipline to one of pure, unfettered self-indulgence. Every day, we're bombarded with advertisements urging us to gratify our desires: "Thirst is everything. Obey your thirst." "Just do it." "Betcha can't eat just one."

These messages influence us, but they can't take away our will to resist. There must be something else—something *inside*—making us susceptible to them. The best way to experience it is to watch what happens when you *do* try to restrain your urges. Try this:

- Put yourself in the state of craving you experienced in the last exercise. Feel the insatiable hunger driving you to get whatever it is you want.
- Now imagine holding back—forbidding yourself from getting what you want.
- Notice what your reaction is: how does it feel to be denied the thing you want so badly?

You may have felt sad, anxious, frustrated, or angry. But whatever you felt, most people are startled at how painful it is to even think about depriving themselves.

It's surprising because logically, you know you'll get over it. If you stop yourself from getting high, having an extra slice of cake, or buying something online, it'll hurt momentarily, but the pain will go away. In a short time, you'll move on and forget you even wanted it. So why is that moment of self-denial so painful?

The answer: Part X has convinced you of a lie: *Being deprived is intolerable. You* can't *get through it.* This isn't a lie you're conscious of. But remember, Part X doesn't work out in the open, where you can fight it with logic. It controls you from your unconscious. On that level, X convinces you that deprivation is a kind of death—something you'll *never* recover from.

If you don't believe this, watch a little kid who's been told he can't have something he wants—it could be a toy, a sugary drink, another ride on your back, or anything else. He's instantly overwhelmed with feelings of intense grief and anxiety. Deep down, he believes the loss is insurmountable.

When you're watching a child in hysterics because he can't watch his favorite TV show, it's easy to maintain perspective: you know he'll live through it and come out the other end. But it's not so easy when *you're* the one being deprived. If you're honest about how hard it is to exercise self-restraint, you'll concede that most of the time Part X, not your rational mind, is controlling your attitude toward deprivation. Its strategy is to flood you with impulses that *override* logic, making it seem as if you'll die if you don't get what you want. That's why you give in without a second thought.

How do you fight the lie that deprivation equals death when you're not even aware of it?

You have to start by taking a different view of deprivation. It isn't what you think it is. Being deprived of something isn't a permanent end point, a death from which you
never recover. It's the opposite. *Deprivation is a portal into
more life.* Not only can you tolerate it, it's the pathway to living more fully than you ever thought possible. Once you can
live through it, deprivation frees you from being enslaved to
your impulses.

But it's not enough to believe this; you have to experience
it. That requires a shift in focus. We normally focus outside
ourselves, on the thing we're depriving ourselves of: sex, a
piece of jewelry, "one last hand" of poker, etc. Even if we're
able to deny ourselves the thing we want, we remain focused
on it, wishing we could have it and feeling robbed of it. This
keeps us fixated on the outside world.

If there's something we crave *outside* us to make us feel
more complete, then it stands to reason there must be something missing *inside* us—an incompleteness or emptiness.
What would happen if we forgot about the thing we want in
the outside world? In fact, what if we forgot about the outside world as a whole, and shifted our focus to this hollow-
ness that exists inside?

What is this void, and why don't we know more about it?
Because Part X has convinced us that to look into the void, or
even to acknowledge it, means we'll be swallowed up by it.
Better to keep filling it up with stuff from outside ourselves.
But in the end, nothing works. That emptiness is always
there, gnawing at our insides.

To liberate yourself from craving, you have to try something different: resist the impulse to escape and simply look, calmly, into the void. You really don't know anything about it (having avoided it your entire life), so be neutral about it. It may surprise you. In fact, when you stare patiently into the inner abyss, you begin to sense something you never would have expected. What felt like a dark, barren, dead zone lights up with life. It's like a womb, pregnant with potential.

Don't try to make logical sense of this, just see if you can experience it for yourself. Try the following exercise:

- Put yourself in the same state of deprivation you created in the last exercise: you want something very badly and you are barred from getting it. Make the feelings of deprivation as intense as you can.
- Now let go of the thing you want. Forget about it completely. As you do, imagine that the entire outside world disappears as well; it's no longer a source of gratification for you.
- Look inside yourself. What was a feeling of deprivation is now a vast empty space.
- Face it. Remain calm and perfectly still. Stay focused on the void and see what happens.

Most of our patients, when they do this exercise, start to sense a stirring, a movement in the void, like there's something down there. Some have to repeat the exercise before the void reveals its true nature. But eventually, the nothingness turns into a something-ness.

This something-ness is your Life Force—an infinite body of fullness and light that contains everything you need to live a meaningful life. This sounds like the stuff of miracles. How it is possible for emptiness to transform itself into fullness? Humankind used to have an intuitive understanding of this. The mystical Jewish tradition of kabbalah teaches that before the creation of the universe, God was everywhere. In order to allow space for the universe to come into being, God had to contract, leaving an empty void. That nothingness was where all of Creation flowered into its full potential. In a similar vein, "Shiva," in the Hindu tradition, is a formless void and, simultaneously, the womb where all things come into being.

What these disparate traditions describe as a cosmic process also occurs inside every human being: there is an inner void in which the seeds of your potential can flower.

Marty didn't care about Hinduism or Jewish mysticism—all he cared about was his son. To have a positive impact on Chad, Marty was going to have to control his temper. That meant he was going to have to face his own void and find a way to fill it.

For Marty, and all of us, that requires a tool.

THE TOOL: THE BLACK SUN

Use this tool at the moment Part X floods you with any kind of self-defeating urge—to reach for ice cream or potato chips, check your email, lose your temper, etc. Used repeatedly, this tool will train you to stop giving in to these impulses and turn inward instead. That's where you'll find an unexpected sense of abundance. Over time, by filling yourself up from the inside, your whole relationship with the outside world will change: you'll be able to bring something *to* the world, rather than trying to extract something *from* it.

The first time through, use the same desire you worked with earlier in the chapter to reproduce the sense of deprivation. As soon as you feel the pain of not getting what you want, walk yourself through the following steps slowly, taking time on each one. You may wish to record the steps on your phone or digital recorder, leaving time between each step. Then close your eyes and listen to your recording.

THE BLACK SUN

DEPRIVATION: Feel the deprivation of not getting what you want, as intensely as possible. Then let go of the thing you want. Forget about the outside world—let it disappear.

EMPTINESS: Look inside yourself. What was a feeling of deprivation is now an endless void. Face it. Remain calm and still.

FULLNESS: From the depths of the void, imagine a Black Sun ascends, expanding inside until you become one with its warm, limitless energy.

GIVING: Redirect your attention to the outside world. The Black Sun energy will overflow, surging out of you. As it enters the world, it becomes a pure, white light of infinite giving.

This tool can free you from one of Part X's most potent weapons—your own impulses. Let's go through it step by step, so you can understand exactly how it works.

The initial act of self-restraint is crucial. It allows you to experience deprivation, which is the first step to learning how to tolerate it. But if you stop there, Part X will keep your attention focused on the thing you want. You'll stay stuck—wanting it and feeling deprived of it. This is what twelve-step groups call "white-knuckling it"—you're fighting your urges but you haven't acknowledged, much less filled, the gaping hole inside you. If hell is being addicted to whatever you want, this is purgatory; you've restrained yourself but you're still empty inside.

To get to heaven, you have to go further and let go of the specific thing you want. Not only that, you have to turn away from the outside world altogether, renouncing hope that anything in it will ever fill you up.

Once you've turned away from the outside world, you're no longer focused on the specific thing you want, so you no longer feel deprived of it. Instead, there's simply a vast emptiness inside you. In the past, you've run away from this void. This time, you're going to face it. If you're patient and calm, it will reveal its secret: far from being empty, it's a space of infinite abundance. It is through this void that your Life Force will enter you.

But the Life Force is formless, diffuse, and in a sense, unknowable. For that reason, civilizations throughout history have found certain symbols for it. These symbols help us understand and, even more important, *experience* the Life Force. The Black Sun is the first of these symbols, but you'll discover others as you learn more of the tools. Your unconscious already knows these symbols—they are buried inside everyone—so upon seeing each symbol, you'll find yourself able to tap into hidden resources at the moment you need them.

If you've seen a solar eclipse, the Black Sun should look something like the moment of "totality," when the moon passes in front of the sun, hiding it. The image might seem strange at first, but the explanation is simple. You were born with a bright and powerful Sun inside you; as an infant, you were filled with the light of its love, only dimly aware of the world outside you. But to thrive, a human being needs to learn how to satisfy its physical needs in the outside world; that's the task of childhood. Part X takes advantage of this and, with the help of our culture, convinces you that the outside world will quench not only your physical needs, but your spiritual ones as well. You turn further and further away from the inner Sun. Like a once-beloved stuffed animal now consigned to the dark corner of a closet, the Sun sinks into the darkness, leaving a void.

What the tool does is reverse this process. It directs your attention away from the outside world—you give it up as a source of fulfillment. You turn inward; you pay attention to the dark void. For many, it's the first time they've ever said, "I'm curious about what's *inside* me." At that moment, the Sun responds by rising back up again. It seems strange that the Sun would be black, but its blackness reminds you that, unwittingly, you have obscured it by trying to fill all your needs in the outside world; you have allowed the outer world to eclipse the inner sun.

As the Black Sun rises, it suffuses your entire being with its infinite warmth. It fills you up so completely you can stop craving things outside you. And when you turn back toward the outside world, you'll naturally find the Black Sun energy overflowing from you and spilling out into the world. This is because the energy of the Black Sun is infinitely expansive; it cannot be contained by anyone or anything. As it enters the world, it reveals its true nature—a pure, white light of infinite giving. The eclipse is over; the Sun shines brightly again, unimpeded by your cravings.

If you look at the overall arc of the tool, you can see its true purpose: it reverses the direction of your energy. We spend most of our lives trying to *pull things in*, based on Part X's lie that these things will fill us up. The tool reverses this. Instead of pulling something in, the tool allows you to *put something out.* This reveals the only real solution to our endless desire to get more: *give more.* Members of twelve-step programs put this principle into action by being of service to others. They're eager to give to others because it helps them overcome their own cravings. If you use the Black Sun tool every time you crave something, you'll experience what most members of these groups do: the more you give, the more you're filled up.

This is one of the great mysteries of being human: how can giving something away make you *more* complete? It seems like a contradiction because we're used to functioning in a finite world. In that world, if I have ten dollars and give you five, I only have five dollars left. Your gain is my loss. But the inner world—the world of the Black Sun—is infinite. If I have an infinite resource inside me, the more I give to you, the more I activate it for myself—we all gain.

How and When to Use the Black Sun

Once you understand the deeper meaning of the tool, we want you to start using it in real life. If you were learning a new piece on the piano, you'd have to practice it over and over. The tools are the same. Practice the Black Sun until you can remember it without struggling. (We've given each step of the tool a name to help you remember it quickly: Deprivation, Emptiness, Fullness, Giving.) The first few times you practice, you'll have to go through each step slowly, but pretty soon you'll get to the point where you can move through the whole tool quickly, in under ten seconds. This tempo is important. Often, you'll be using the tool in the middle of a busy day. If it takes too long, you won't use it at all.

Likewise, don't start with the impulses that are hardest for you to control. If you overeat, trying to learn the tool in front of an all-you-can-eat buffet is a setup for failure. Instead, start with small temptations or just imagine a temptation you might have to face in the next twenty-four hours. Self-control is like a muscle; if you build it up on smaller temptations, you'll eventually be much more successful at tackling the larger ones.

Once you've learned *how* to use the tool, the question becomes *when* to use it. For each of the four tools in this book, there's a set of easily recognizable moments that call for its use. We call these "cues," just like a cue that prompts an actor to say his lines. Use the tool immediately every time you recognize a cue.

For the Black Sun tool, the most obvious cue occurs the moment you feel the impulse to act. You're about to look at cute kitten videos instead of working. You're on the verge of reacting to someone in a way that'll start a fight. You feel the impulse to put yourself down. It's important that you use the Black Sun immediately when you recognize one of these cues. Impulses gain momentum very rapidly, so the faster you use the tool, the more effective it will be.

Speed is important for another reason: it gives you less time to think. Thinking doesn't help you control your impulses; in fact, you'll find that the more you try to think your way out of an impulse, the more Part X will flood you with rationalizations for why you should get what you want. "Just this once won't hurt," "You've had a tough day, you deserve it," "You've already blown it today, you can start trying tomorrow," and so on. There's only one thing that will help you fight your impulses, and it isn't thinking. It's the power of the Black Sun rising and filling you up from within.

There's another cue to use the Black Sun tool, though it's more subtle and requires a little more effort to identify. For much of our waking life, we're not actually indulging our impulses; instead, we're looking forward to the moment when we'll get to give in. A pothead will spend his workday fantasizing about firing up a joint as soon as he gets home. A writer will get himself to work on a difficult assignment with the promise he can watch porn as soon as he's finished. A teenager will get through a boring class imagining the outfit she's going to buy after school.

Every time you indulge one of these fantasies, you make it more likely you'll act on your impulses in the future. In a way, each fantasy is a little preview of the pleasure to come— a self-invented "promo" for self-indulgence.

Use the Black Sun as soon as you recognize yourself slipping into one of these self-gratifying visions. This is a slightly different use of the tool. You're using it to restrain your thoughts, not your actions. Stressed at work, when the pothead starts to fantasize about getting high, he'd use the tool instead. Resisting his assignment, when the writer starts to imagine his pornographic reward, he'd use the Black Sun. Bored at school, as soon as the teen starts to daydream about the dress, she'd cut off the daydream with the tool.

Whether you're using the Black Sun to fight an impulse to do something now or the fantasy of giving in to it in the future, don't feel like a failure if you have to use the tool more than once. Remember, Part X doesn't give up easily. Keep using the tool, over and over again, until the impulse (or fantasy) dies down. Even if Part X wins a battle here or there, you've demonstrated you're never going to let it take over without a fight.

The Black Sun in Real Life

For Marty, Chad's slide into videogame addiction provided a huge incentive to work on himself. The blustering bully I'd met in the first session was now painfully aware of what a bad role model he'd been. If he wanted to learn to restrain his temper, he had to accept what that meant: using a tool to stop himself whenever he felt like raging at anyone.

The moment I taught him the Black Sun, I could see that Marty was dubious about the whole idea of using tools. "I don't know, Doc. . . . I once had a girlfriend who thought she could get parking spaces by visualizing them. I kidded her about it every time we circled the block looking for one."

"Did you kid her or scream at her?" I asked. He turned red. "Seriously, Marty, you're not exactly an expert on self-control, so don't pretend you know what's going to help. I know the tool sounds strange, but at least try it and see what happens."

Fortunately, he was desperate enough to take a chance.

He wasn't disappointed. He used the Black Sun the moment he felt the impulse to take his anger out on anybody. As you can imagine, he had to use it quite a bit—when he was stuck in traffic, when his assistant bungled a phone call, when he was waiting on line at Starbucks, and so on. It didn't always work, especially in the beginning, but I had warned him to ignore the inevitable failures and just keep going. His relationship with his son hanging in the balance, he had no other choice.

Then something unprecedented happened. Susan and Ashley had a fight without him. Susan noticed cash missing from her wallet and immediately accused her daughter of stealing. Ashley claimed her mother had paid it to the plumber that afternoon. Her exact words were, "You're fucking senile, Mom." As the family descended into chaos, Marty felt the usual urge to end it all with a tantrum. Instead, he used the Black Sun tool over and over. "It was the weirdest thing. I felt calm even though they were screaming at each other."

Then he noticed Chad slink off to his room. "I tried to use the tool a couple more times, but I couldn't get my mind off of what he was doing in his room. I followed him there, and sure enough, he was playing on his iPad." Marty demanded to know what the hell Chad was doing playing videogames when he had a precalculus exam the next day.

Chad's reply: "Dad . . . don't you have a poker game you're late for?"

Needless to say, Marty went ballistic. This pattern—making progress and then falling back into bad habits—is very common. You should expect it when you start to work on yourself. You'll take a step forward, as Marty did by staying out of the argument between his wife and his daughter, and then you'll take a step backward. This pattern makes sense if you remember that Part X never gives up. When you achieve some degree of mastery over your worst impulses, Part X will work even harder to flood you with new ones.

Now, because of Chad's disrespect, Part X had given Marty a new excuse to stop using the Black Sun altogether. "Can you believe the way he spoke to me?" Marty fumed. "No way am I putting up with that kind of disrespect. If I'd ever talked to my father that way, he would've smacked me across the room!"

"Yeah? How did that work out in terms of teaching you to control yourself?" Marty was taken aback. "Seriously, you did a great job with your wife and daughter. It was a huge breakthrough. But if you want Chad to learn self-control, you're going to have to do something your father *didn't* do— control yourself with him too."

I wanted Marty to go all the way on this—learn to control himself in the face of any provocation. So I decided to take advantage of the mistake he'd made with Chad and turn it into a learning opportunity. I directed Marty to close his eyes and conjure the memory of Chad's insolence as vividly as he could, as if it were happening right now. His face reddened and he clenched his fists as he relived Chad's insolence.

"That's good," I said. "Now use the Black Sun tool. Use it as many times as you have to until you calm down." Gradually, I could see his anger abate. When he opened his eyes, his breathing had slowed; he seemed at peace.

You should try this whenever you make the mistake of giving in to an impulse: you sneak an extra slice of cake, duck out of confronting somebody, start texting a friend in the middle of work. These "mistakes" are excellent *ex post facto* opportunities to learn self-restraint. All you need to do is use the tool retrospectively, in your imagination. The more you do this, the more you'll build up the strength to resist the next temptation you're faced with.

But Marty was still deeply concerned about his son. "Look, I get it. Whatever I do, it can't be out of rage. But in the meantime, my son's becoming an addict. If I'm not on him, who's going to make him stop?"

"Nobody's going to *make* him stop. Chad's going to choose to stop, with your help. But we're not at that stage yet, because he won't accept your help until he looks up to you, which means you have to become a model of self-control. So guess what? We want to expand your use of the tool. He's obviously aware of your gambling problem, so now I want you to use the tool not only when you're about to lose your temper, but also whenever you get the urge to go out gaming."

Marty shot me a look that, as a shrink, I've grown accustomed to: he hated me. But he also knew I was right. He wasn't convinced that Chad would ever accept his help, but he was determined to try. He kept on using the Black Sun, not only when he felt like raging but also when he wanted to go gambling. A few weeks later, a miracle happened. Chad passed Marty's bedroom and did a double take—his father wasn't out at the card clubs, he was reading in bed. Despite himself, Chad smiled at his father. Marty told me at our next session, "It's the first time he's smiled at me in months!"

Under strict orders from me, Marty continued to lay off his anti–videogame campaign and just tried to listen to Chad. Gradually, his son opened up to him. He told Marty that he gave up on school because no matter how well he did, his father was always yelling at him about something. The video-games started as a way to screen out the family fights and quickly became a habit. Eventually, the two of them reached a compromise: Chad would get his homework done first, then he could play videogames for an hour.

This worked out better than anyone expected. Chad learned how to regulate his own self-sabotaging impulses, and Marty learned that it was the quieter, noncontrolling version of himself that had the greatest impact on everyone around him.

But life always presents new challenges. As Marty and Chad were growing in their relationship, Susan was growing in another way. Her late night binges were completely out of control. To his credit, Marty had developed such faith in the Black Sun that he restrained the urge to criticize her. This was completely out of character for Marty, who'd always taken potshots at her whenever he could. As Susan began to reflect on this change—and how content Marty seemed—she assumed the worst. One evening, she burst into their bedroom in tears. "Are you having an affair?"

Marty was dumbfounded. He'd never spent so much time at home. He wanted to defend himself, but he used the Black Sun. He took a deep breath and asked her, gently, what was going on. Susan admitted that she felt threatened by how much he'd changed. "You seem so much more confident. Why would you want to be with a fatty like me?"

Marty reassured her that he loved her regardless of her weight. "But I hate to see you so down on yourself. The shrink gave me a tool for controlling my temper. Maybe you should use it whenever you want to eat." To the surprise of both of them, Susan was willing. It took him five minutes to teach her the Black Sun tool. That night, she was able to walk away from an unfinished gallon of ice cream. She had a million more questions about the Black Sun, but Marty insisted she make an appointment with me. "It's dangerous for me to work on anybody but myself."

When Susan came to my office, the first thing she wanted to talk about was how much Marty had changed. "Are you sure you haven't substituted a look-alike for my husband, minus the anger gene? How did he get to be so much more confident?"

It doesn't seem like self-restraint would increase your confidence, but it does. Think about it for a moment: what would your life be like if you gave in to every urge that came into your head? You'd be living on shaky ground, knowing your life could fall off the rails at any moment. You wouldn't be able to rely on commitments you'd made to yourself. It would destroy your confidence in yourself. In contrast, when you can restrain yourself, *you*—instead of your urges—are in the driver's seat. You control your choices. This gives you a sense of confidence that the most important things in your life aren't going to be sacrificed on a whim, or because an urge suddenly seizes hold of you.

But it was Marty's newfound calm that affected Susan the most. "I used to be on high alert all the time, like I was living in a combat zone, getting ready for the next explosion." Then she looked perplexed. "I don't understand why, but the calmer he is, the easier it is for me to work on my weight problem. I've said no to food before, but in the back of my mind, I always knew it wouldn't last. I don't know why, but this time I feel like I'll be able to do it."

This is another great benefit of self-control. Not only do you gain confidence in yourself, you also have a profoundly uplifting effect on the people around you. Because they no longer have to protect themselves from your bad habits, they can start to take responsibility for their own.

We are all connected. We can't help having an impact on one another, for good or for ill. When they first came to see me, Marty and Susan were a good example of two people bringing out the worst in each other. Every time Marty lost his temper, Susan's Part X would use it against her: "See, he's not on your side. No one is. You're trapped: your daughter steals from you, your husband screams at you, and then he abandons you for the card clubs. And it's *never* going to change. C'mon, follow me to the freezer. That sweet, velvety ice cream will make you feel better." Similarly, every time Susan conspired to keep her daughter's secrets, Marty's Part X would take over: "Your daughter's already a thief, and now your wife is turning her into a liar. You've got to shake some sense into them *now!*"

But human beings are also connected in positive ways. When they fight Part X in themselves, the Life Force they generate spills out to the people around them. Now that Marty's temper and gambling were under control, Susan was feeling less alone and more supported. "For the first time, it feels like Marty's on my side, like he wants the best for me and our family." As a consequence, Part X was finding it harder to convince Susan that her secret late night binges were her only pleasure in life. "Also," Susan admitted, "after Marty worked so hard to use the Black Sun tool, I would feel ashamed if I didn't work as hard on myself." Marty had started the ball rolling, and now Susan felt it was possible for her to become a catalyst for even further change in their family.

Part X can spread from person to person like a crippling virus, damaging the potential of every single person in a family. But the opposite is also true. When parents are committed to using the tools, the Life Force they evoke can free them and everyone else in a family.

In a few months, Marty and Susan had become experts in using the Black Sun on their own problems. As a result, Chad was back on track. Now they were ready to deal with Ashley's problems. One day, as Susan was going over the credit card bills, she discovered her daughter had bought a dress on a credit card she was supposed to use only for emergencies. Susan described what happened next. "First, I felt the urge to talk to Ashley on my own. That's the way I used to handle it to avoid Marty's temper tantrums. But I used the Black Sun several times and went to Marty first."

Amazingly, it was a real discussion, not a blame fest. "Then we sat down with Ashley and told her how disappointed we were. We told her the dress money was coming out of her allowance, plus a penalty for misusing the credit card." Ashley did what most kids do—told them they'd ruined her life. She also barraged them with excuses, tried to pit them against each other, and (as a last resort) blamed it all on a friend of hers. Both Susan and Marty were tempted to get into an argument with her. Instead, spontaneously, they both closed their eyes and used the Black Sun right in front of their daughter. "You know what we did then?" Susan smiled. "We held hands and walked away from her. She was speechless."

It was the first time Marty and Susan had acted in concert—a huge step forward for them. But I cautioned them—they would have to *continue* to use the Black Sun and present a united front. Kids who grow up without any leadership rebel against it when it's initially introduced. True to form, Ashley found ingenious ways of testing their authority. She found her mother's password to an online store and bought an outfit for herself, hoping they wouldn't catch it. She tried to ignite one of Marty's temper tantrums by buying a gallon of Susan's favorite ice cream and telling Marty it was Susan's secret stash. She even tried to get Chad to break the videogame rules he'd agreed to. Marty and Susan weren't perfect—no parent is—but they were determined to continue using the Black Sun every time they were tempted to overreact or turn against each other. Eventually, Ashley got used to the new regime.

By this time, Marty and Susan no longer needed to see me weekly—they consulted me alone or together on an as-needed basis. I finally knew they no longer needed me when they came in together for a final session. Susan was beaming. "I went into Ashley's room the other night and you'll never guess what she was doing: researching schools that specialize in fashion and design. She seems to have a flair for it."

It was so fitting (excuse the bad pun): Ashley, the ultimate consumer of fashion, would go on to become a *creator* of fashion. The Black Sun had helped everyone in the family free themselves of the self-indulgent habits they'd grown addicted to—clearing the way for each to fulfill his or her potential.

Children and Part X

As Chad and Ashley illustrate, adults are not the only ones who have a Part X. X tries to gain a foothold in children as early as it can, creating bad habits that will squelch the child's potential for a lifetime. There are myriad examples: a young child gets into the habit of taking things that aren't hers or hitting other kids; an older child gets into the habit of texting, watching TV, or playing videogames at times when he should be learning to interact with other people; a teen gets into the habit of lying about where she is, or about whether there's adult supervision at a party.

None of these misdeeds would be significant if they happened once in a while. But Part X will always try to turn them into long-term habits. If Chad had continued to give up on school for the pleasure of videogaming, or if Ashley continued to steal and lie, it would have seriously compromised their future as adults.

When faced with a child who's acting out, most parents don't want to work on themselves; they want a remedy that will work quickly to solve the problem. This is understandable, and there is an entire industry built on parenting advice, full of specialists whose books recommend techniques and methods you can try. And most of them would work if it weren't for the child's Part X.

But Part X is contemptuous of these techniques. It's paying attention to something much bigger: how much self-control you have, as a parent. If you indulge your impulses, X will convince your kids to do the same. You might be thinking, "But I hide my drinking, pornography, overspending, etc." But you don't hide it as well as you think you do. I can't count the number of kids I've interviewed who know *exactly* what their parents are doing "in secret." But what's more confounding is that kids have a sixth sense about parents. Even if you successfully hide the details, they'll still sense that you're living self-indulgently, and take that as an endorsement of their worst impulses. Marty lectured his family every night about self-discipline, but it wasn't until he started *living* a self-disciplined life that everyone sat up and took notice.

So when parents ask me how they can help their children control their impulses, my response is always the same: control your own, as diligently and consistently as you possibly can. That's how Susan and Marty were able to gain traction with their kids. They worked to restrain themselves first, and once they'd mastered their own impulses they set limits on Chad's videogaming and on Ashley's spending. The limits worked because the overall ethos in the family had shifted from self-indulgence to self-control.

Our culture doesn't help parents in this regard. Our children are bombarded with a tsunami of images—in advertising, movies, and online—depicting adulthood as a free buffet of expensive clothing, fast cars, no-strings-attached sexuality, mind-altering drugs, alcohol, and so on. Children have a normal, healthy desire to grow into adults, but Part X takes advantage of the way adulthood is portrayed, enticing kids with the promise of *self-indulgence*. Essentially, our culture has allied itself with Part X, encouraging our children to *give in to*, rather than *resist*, their worst impulses.

That doesn't mean it's hopeless. It simply means that parents have to work even harder to create a different culture within their families. Every time a parent uses a tool to control their worst impulses, they send a powerful message of hope to the entire family: *change is possible*. That message of hope encourages everyone in the family to try to change themselves. That's how Marty was able to bring about a shift in the family dynamic: Susan became willing to work on her weight, Chad became willing to limit his gaming, and Ashley developed an interest in creating, rather than merely consuming, fashion.

This isn't just an abstract theory. Test it out for yourself. Use the Black Sun every time you want to act out impulsively. Keep doing it no matter how difficult the circumstances become. You'll see the behavior of the people around you improve. By using the Black Sun tool, you will generate a force that not only helps you control yourself, but becomes part of the fabric of your relationships, family, and larger community.

Transforming Death into Life

The Black Sun gives you access to the Life Force at the very moment when Part X is trying to steal it from you. Remember, Part X works under the radar, siphoning your gas tank one drop at a time—you waste your energy on petty impulses that excite you in the short run but drain your life of purpose in the long run. The Black Sun gives you the power to restrain yourself, preventing the liquid gold from going down the drain.

But self-restraint isn't just a defensive maneuver to *conserve* your Life Force; it actually *increases* it. When you restrain an impulse, the energy doesn't just disappear—it changes its nature. The following is a picture of how this happens inside you:

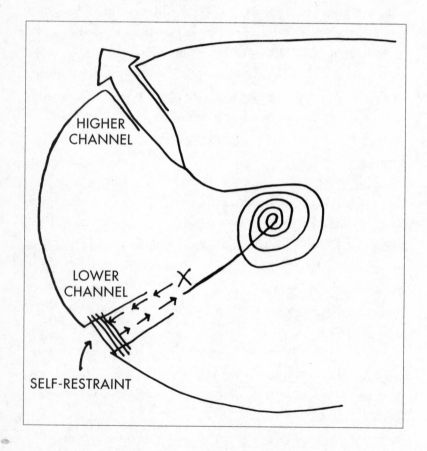

HIGHER
CHANNEL

LOWER
CHANNEL

X

SELF-RESTRAINT

Starting at the lower left-hand part of the picture, you can see that Part X is generating a self-gratifying impulse, represented by the small arrows moving out from "X." The impulse moves into the outside world, through what is labeled the "Lower Channel." When you act impulsively, you're reaching through this channel into the outside world to take something in—hoping it will fill you up. What really happens when you indulge the impulse is that the energy pours out of you, leaving you with less than you started with. When you use the Black Sun tool to restrain yourself, you create a barrier that closes off the lower channel. In the picture, this barrier is labeled "Self-Restraint" and is depicted as four solid lines at the mouth of the lower channel. When the impulse generated by X hits this barrier, it is forced to reverse direction and go back inside you.

That's when the magic begins. Whenever you hold an impulse back, its nature changes. In the picture, that's represented by the lines going around and around in the area of your heart. The heart, much more than the head, can transform energy, and it does this without your being aware of it. Eventually, this transformed energy goes back out into the world, only this time it goes through what we call a "higher" channel (at the upper left-hand part of the picture.) There's a big difference between this energy and the impulse you started with. The energy that pours out of the higher channel is abundant, and increases by giving itself away. We depict this by making the arrow wider and fuller. As you know from the tool, the giving energy is the only thing that can fill you up.

This leads to a more profound understanding of what self-restraint really is. It's about much more than simply controlling your behavior. It's about transforming lower, greedy energy into higher, giving energy. You start with the impulse energy of Part X, and you end up with more Life Force.

In a strange, mysterious way, you're transforming death into life. Obviously, we're not talking about literal, physical death; rather, the kind of "living death" Part X tries to create— a life defined by a sense of tedium, monotony, and meaninglessness. One of the most effective ways Part X can turn your life into a living death is to get you to act on impulses. Although they're exciting at first, eventually they drain your life of anything new or meaningful. Texting, cruising the Internet, overeating, smoking, etc., all become repetitive habits. The more you yield to these impulses, the more you live like a machine, performing the same meaningless operations over and over again, with no freedom of choice or awareness of what you're doing. That's the definition of a living death.

The Black Sun tool changes all that. It takes the deadening energy of Part X and transmutes it into more Life Force. This isn't just theoretical; you actually feel it happening inside of you. If you use the tool enough times, you'll feel yourself taking hold of your self-gratifying urges and molding them, like a lump of clay, into the infinite giving-ness of the Life Force. There's a sublime sense of excitement and accomplishment that comes with mastering this alchemy of transforming negative into positive energy. Each of the tools in this book has the same, reanimating effect. When you use them repeatedly, you breathe life—infinite forces of change, newness, and vitality—into yourself.

FREQUENTLY ASKED QUESTIONS

When I use the tool, I get to step three, Fullness, but the Black Sun doesn't appear. Why does that happen and how can I get it to show up?

Don't worry if the Black Sun doesn't automatically appear in step three of the tool. It's common for that to happen, especially when you're learning the tool for the first time. You're so used to filling your needs in the outside world, that without realizing it, you've rejected the Black Sun for most of your life. For it to appear, you have to create an empty space, and you can't do that without acknowledging how painful it is to be deprived of what you want.

The answer is to go back over the first two steps of the tool slowly—allowing yourself to feel the pain they create. In step one, Deprivation, you should feel deprived, anxious, frustrated—you can't get what you want. Feel these feelings as intensely as you can. Then make the pain even worse by letting go of the whole outside world as a source—nothing there will *ever* fill you up inside. That should feel like an even greater loss. Then, when you turn inward in step two, Emptiness, you'll feel the gaping emptiness inside yourself; its what's left after you deny yourself what you want in the outside world. Stay focused on the void; wait patiently, and don't try to make anything happen. If you're truly willing to go through the discomfort of these two steps, the Black Sun will emerge on its own.

I've been able to control my impulses just through self-discipline. When I want something and I know it isn't good for me, I don't let myself have it. You seem to be implying that that's not enough. Why?

It's great that you have the willpower to control your behavior, but we want you to go beyond that. It's important for you to experience something most people never face—the vast emptiness that's inside of you. Understandably, most people don't see the value in that—they run away from it. They think their job is done as long as they can control themselves.

But confronting the abyss inside yourself is of the utmost importance. It's the only way to discover that *it isn't empty*! It's filled with infinite life. When you experience this—again and again—it changes your whole life. You begin to see yourself as someone who can bring something *to* the world, rather than needing something *from* it. Life becomes less about *controlling* your urges, and more about transmuting them into something higher: the power of giving.

You mentioned "the devil in his role as 'tempter.'" Are you asking me to accept the devil as a real being, with horns, a pointy beard, and a leering grin?

No, we're not asking you to believe in the devil as a real being. But it's a useful metaphor because almost everyone has been exposed to the concept, whether they choose to believe it's real or not.

Throughout history, the devil has been seen as tempting mankind, step by step, down the path of self-destruction. That's exactly how Part X uses impulses. Whether it seduces you with pornography, drinking too much, or constantly checking social media, each impulse in itself seems innocuous. But the more you give in, the harder it is to resist. Eventually you pay the ultimate price: it's too late to live the life you could have lived. You don't have to call it the devil, but it's in your best interests to acknowledge that that's a dangerous force—and it's inside everyone.

You seem to be advocating a completely ascetic existence. Am I never supposed to enjoy life?

Of course you are! We are not encouraging you to live a Spartan existence, devoid of pleasure or satisfaction. But most people think that gratifying their impulses is going to bring them pleasure. It's the opposite: if you examine the lives of people who gratify their every whim, they're desperately *unhappy*. They spend most of their time looking for the next fix, and over the long run nothing satisfies them. The classic addict is someone who's had one peak experience, spends the rest of his life trying to re-create it—and in the end, fails.

We need a new understanding of what gives us pleasure. As strange as it sounds, the greatest satisfactions in life come from giving out—pouring yourself into people and projects—rather than getting your immediate needs gratified. That's why we can say with confidence that if you use the Black Sun tool, your life will be *more* enjoyable than it's ever been before.

OTHER USES OF THE BLACK SUN

THE BLACK SUN ENABLES YOU TO BEAR DOWN AND FOCUS ON ONE THING AT A TIME, WITHOUT GIVING IN TO DISTRACTIONS. It's difficult for some people to stay focused and see a task through to completion; they lose interest as soon as what they're doing becomes tedious or repetitive. This makes it difficult for them to complete tasks. Worse, it alienates other people—they end up feeling ignored or even snubbed when they aren't getting the distracted person's full attention. This has become a huge problem in our society. Because we crave constant stimulation, we get distracted while driving, taking care of kids, even in the middle of conversations. In a sense, it's as if the whole society is infected with Attention Deficit Disorder.

David was a successful talent agent. Motivated by the thrill of the chase, he was particularly adept at signing big-name talent—actors, writers, directors, and so on. His quick wit and winning style made him a natural. His problem was that once he signed a client and the real work began, he lost interest. He couldn't sit still long enough to read through an entire script; at staff meetings, he would get bored and start checking his phone; on important phone calls with clients, he would surreptitiously watch videos on his computer. Needless to say, he was even worse at home, taking phone calls in the middle of his kids' bedtime routine, and barely acknowledging his wife as they turned in for the night.

The reckoning came when he was fired by his biggest client. They had been friends since childhood, so it was a huge personal loss. But it also represented a lucrative chunk of business and was a blow to his standing within the agency. Horrified, he begged the client for an explanation. The client was blunt: "Do you think I don't hear your keyboard clacking away when I'm on the phone with you? You make me feel like I'm an interruption instead of your friend and client. I deserve an agent who makes me feel like I'm the only thing that matters." David pleaded with his friend to give him one more chance. "Put me on probation if you want to, but at least give me the opportunity to change." The client gave him three months.

David started to use the Black Sun tool every time he got bored and wanted instant stimulation: checking out other women while at a restaurant with his wife, answering his phone while playing with his kid, responding to emails in the middle of a staff meeting. At first, he found it very frustrating to stick with whatever he was doing, and there were many lapses. But gradually, he found his attention span increasing. He knew he had passed the test when his client took him out to dinner. At the end of the meal, the client smiled and said, "I feel like I have my agent back, and more important, my friend."

THE BLACK SUN GIVES YOU PEACE OF MIND WHILE YOU'RE WAITING TO HEAR HOW SOMETHING IMPORTANT WILL TURN OUT.

Life is full of uncertainties. Often, there's nothing we can do but sit tight and wait for the information we

> need to take the next step. Waiting—for the answer
> to a job application, the results of a medical exam,
> or a reply text from someone you have a crush on—
> can feel unbearable. Most of us think, "If only I
> could get the information, then I'd be at peace."
> What we don't realize is that information is like a
> drug—the more you need it, the less peace of mind
> you have.

Sarah had a hard time waiting for anything. "When my son was a high school senior, I would check the mailbox five times a day for letters from colleges." Now that he was a freshman out of state, she desperately wanted to hear from him, but her repetitive texting was driving him away; his replies were getting less frequent and more brusque. But her relationship with her son was only one area where she was couldn't tolerate uncertainty. She applied for a business loan to start a clothing line but found the wait intolerable. "I couldn't stop myself from calling the loan officer. He finally hung up on me."

I told her to start using the Black Sun tool every time she had to deal with uncertainty: wishing her son would contact her; wanting confirmation about social plans that were up in the air; waiting for the doctor's office to give her the results of an MRI. It wasn't always easy and it didn't always work. But gradually she found herself letting go and relaxing; she began to experience a kind of tranquility she'd never known. And there was a bonus. One morning, she woke up to a completely unsolicited text from her son: "Miss u! :-)"

THE BLACK SUN ALLOWS YOU TO STOP SPENDING SO MUCH TIME ON LESS IMPORTANT TASKS AND PUT YOUR ENERGY INTO WHAT REALLY MATTERS THE MOST. Most of us have no idea how much we could accomplish with our lives and the positive impact we could have on the people around us. Part X wants to keep it that way by making inessential, trivial tasks seem more important than the things that matter most in life. As a result, we come to the end of our lives never having fulfilled our true purpose. Oliver Wendell Holmes expressed it elegiacally: "Alas for those that never sing, / But die with all their music in them!"

No one would ever have accused Nicole of not doing her duty. She ran the most efficient, well-organized household any of her friends had ever seen. Her kids were always up, dressed, and fed in time for carpool. By the end of the day, every toy was put away, every dish washed, every newspaper recycled. When Nicole walked into a room, she had an uncanny ability to spot anything out of place—a TV remote left on the wrong table, a crooked wall hanging, a book tipped to its side instead of upright—and it was immediately corrected.

To the outside world, her life seemed perfect, the envy of her friends. Only her husband knew the truth. An English teacher, he knew that Nicole's secret longing was to write poetry. And he had the chops to realize she was gifted. "She'll never show me anything she's written, but every once in a while I sneak into her computer and take a peek. It's the most beautifully expressed, heartrending poetry I've ever read. I just wish I could get her to be less duty-bound and write more."

The natural time for her to write was at the end of the day. But that's when Nicole had her "rituals": the mail had to be sorted, each bill had to be paid immediately, and all phone calls, emails, and texts had to be answered before bedtime. Nicole could not tolerate leaving any of these responsibilities undone. And so, night after night, her poetry was postponed.

Then fate intervened. Nicole's father had been sick for a long time, and the nurses called her to say he was dying. She rushed to his bedside and was with him when he passed. The last thing he said to her was, "I just wish I hadn't worried so much about the little things. I could have done so much more with my life."

It was exactly the wake-up call she needed. She made a commitment to carve out one hour at the end of every day and devote it to writing poetry, come hell or high water. She used the Black Sun to allow her to do this. Every time she thought of a responsibility she was neglecting—a phone call, an unfolded towel, a dish in the sink—she used the Black Sun to resist the temptation to interrupt her writing. It allowed her to let go of the things that didn't matter, and tend to the things that did. Over time, she began to feel a sense of creative fulfillment that a compulsively neat and organized life could never have given her.

SUMMARY

HOW PART X ATTACKS YOU: *It floods you with the impulse to gratify yourself. These urges are so strong they override your ability to assess the consequences of your actions.*

HOW THIS DEADENS YOU: *Giving in to an impulse here or there won't destroy you. But if you keep giving in, little by little Part X shifts the whole purpose of your life. You become devoted to the pursuit of short-term pleasure rather than long-term potential. Eventually, you're left with neither; every urge becomes a repetitive habit, devoid of the original excitement it once held.*

HOW PART X TRICKS YOU INTO GIVING IN: *It convinces you, on an unconscious level, that deprivation is intolerable, the equivalent of death.*

THE SOLUTION: *The Black Sun, used repeatedly, allows you to tolerate deprivation. You discover that being deprived of what you want doesn't kill you. In fact, passing through deprivation makes it possible for you to fulfill your potential. Whatever you want to accomplish— write a book, build a business, be an effective parent—it becomes possible because your impulses no longer divert you from your path.*

Chapter Four

The Tool: The Vortex

Phil explains how using the Vortex gives you
access to unlimited energy if you are
overwhelmed, exhausted, and feel like you lack
the energy to move forward in life.

Beth entered my office for her first session
without looking at me. Her focus was on the furniture. Her
eyes darted around the room until she found the most comfortable chair, which she promptly lowered herself into. She
had the exhausted look of someone who'd been on her feet all
day. I moved toward her to introduce myself, but she waved
me off.

I stood immobile in the middle of my office, feeling like
a lamppost. A moment later, she looked up and said, "I'm
sorry. Give me a minute." She sank back into the chair for a
few more seconds of refueling. Then, grimacing as if she
were moving a huge weight, she pulled herself erect in the
chair.

She explained, "I didn't mean to be rude. I'm drained. I

just needed a little time to get it together." I nodded to show I understood and she broke out in a relieved smile.

"What drained you?" I asked.

"My life. I can't keep up with it. I have to take care of so many people. I try, but I can't please everyone . . . or anyone."

"What do you mean?" I asked her. She audibly sighed. I could see her sizing me up, asking herself if it was worth the effort to explain to me what she'd already explained to a million other doctors, shrinks, and assorted healers, not one of whom understood what she was feeling. Nonetheless, a good sport, she made the effort yet again to explain how it felt to be her.

"What if every one of your patients demanded your attention at the same time?"

"Are you a therapist?" I asked her, feeling stupider and stupider.

"Worse. I'm a caterer. And no matter how demanding your clients are, they can't compare to mine. Yours are just concerned with their mental health. Mine have much more important things to focus on, like which brand of vodka to stock the bar with or the exact shade of white for the tablecloths." She laughed, but it was a gallows laugh.

"What are you laughing at?"

"The way I fool my customers. It feels like I'm holding the whole operation together with Scotch tape. It's just a matter of time before they discover I'm a fraud. I make them think I'm around for the whole event, but I usually arrive late or leave early. I don't have the strength to stay there the whole time. The more face-to-face time I have with clients, the more they'll ask me to do."

"What if they need something important while you're gone?"

"My partner, Eileen, handles it. She has ten times the energy I have; she's also my sister—although it's hard to believe we're from the same family. She's always telling me to 'break through my blocks'—that tiredness is all in my head. It sounds like something she heard in spin class."

Beth smiled but she couldn't hide her annoyance. "Believe me, the exhaustion isn't in my head. Wait until Eileen has a child and a husband, then we'll see if she thinks it's in her head."

Beth had been worked up medically several times. They found nothing. Still, the clear and passionate way she described her problem made me believe her. On the other hand, I'd treated many women (and men for that matter) who, like Beth, were raising children while holding down very demanding jobs. They felt worn out at times, but few of them described the kind of bone-tired weariness that afflicted Beth on a daily basis.

"If it's not 'in your head,' why are you here?"

"It's my daughter," she said, then choked up for a moment. "She says I don't care about her. She won't let me put her to bed. She won't even let me in her room. My husband says it's because I don't spend enough time with her. I love her, but no one gets how exhausted I am by the end of the day. Some days I don't have the strength to walk up the stairs to her room."

"Your husband doesn't believe you?"

"He's got his own ax to grind. He complains that I'm selfish, but he makes me like that. The moment I get home, he follows me around like a puppy demanding attention. Paying attention to him is like dumping my energy into a black hole. He always wants more."

THE PROBLEM: YOU JUST DON'T HAVE ENOUGH ENERGY

As I learned Beth's story, it became clear that she hadn't started out this way. As a child and adolescent, things came easily to her. Blessed with an overflow of God-given talent, she got good grades without much effort. She was one of the "in" girls at school that everyone wanted to hang out with. She was a born athlete, the star of the soccer team. She assumed this charmed life would continue.

It didn't. When she was seventeen, her mother died suddenly. The care of her father—a hopeless alcoholic—fell mostly on her. The physical demands of taking care of him were taxing enough, but the added stress of dealing with his demeaning, angry personality seemed to drain her of her last drop of energy.

"He was like, 'Cook me a steak! Bring me a drink! Clear the table!' Not that he'd ever say 'Thank you.' He was a bloodsucker. All I got was a lot of criticism." She felt the pressure of his demands every moment. "I could hear his voice in my head even when he wasn't around."

Afraid his relentlessness would overwhelm her, she tried to conserve her energy, pulling back from anything that seemed nonessential. That included her friends; she feared they would look at her new role as a servant as being uncool. The young woman who rushed enthusiastically to practice each day had disappeared. She ended up quitting the team, to the dismay of her coach.

She did just enough studying to get by. The moment the school day was over, she'd head directly home, wait on her father, clean the house, and then retreat to her room, where she'd collapse onto her bed for a nap. "I looked forward to the naps. The only time I felt good was when I was asleep."

None of it worked—her fatigue worsened. What was going on? The easy assumption would be to attribute her fatigue to a depression—the result of losing her mother. But if the basic problem is depression, it comes first—fatigue is secondary. Beth was depleted first—if she was depressed it was a reaction to this.

Beth didn't realize that the amount of energy you have depends on your relationship with the world. You create energy when you engage with the world, and you destroy energy when you withdraw from the world. Each time Beth canceled an activity or refused to answer a text message, she didn't protect her energy reserves, she squandered them.

It was as if she was in a boat that was sinking. Her instinct was to throw everything overboard to keep it afloat. But what she was really throwing off the boat were her connections to the world. That made the boat sink faster.

The sister she ended up in business with, Eileen, wasn't as bright or popular as Beth. If life's elevator took Beth to the top floor, it dropped Eileen off in the basement and made her walk up. Eileen expected life to put obstacles in her path and was willing to struggle through them. When their mother died, Eileen stayed connected to friends and relatives, got a part-time job, and sought out mentors.

When Beth stepped into my office, fifteen years had passed since her mother's death, yet her instinct to withdraw from the world still defined her life. What had started out as a survival strategy had become an ingrained habit. She was locked in a cage of her own making.

Happiness is the product of pursuing what's most meaningful to you with complete commitment. If you lack the energy to pursue this goal, happiness is impossible. Have you ever met a happy person who can't get off the couch and engage with the world?

PART X WEAPONIZES FATIGUE

Creating the future you want takes a lot of energy. Without it, your goals feel impossible. Lack of energy is perhaps Part X's most lethal weapon. When you're exhausted it's hard to imagine escaping from the limited life you're living.

Why did Beth end up in this energetically crippled group while Eileen did not? Because Part X tricked her into crippling herself; and it did it under the guise of being protective. The concerned voice telling her she needed a nap, or that she could blow off a friend or skip soccer practice, was Part X whispering in her ear, telling her that life's demands, even the most ordinary, were overwhelming. Years later, preparing a meal, going out with her husband to see a movie, meeting a new customer still felt impossible.

When an inner voice tells you that you've tried hard enough and you deserve a break, Part X is appealing to the most basic human weakness: laziness. When X repeats over and over "You don't have to do this, you don't have the strength," it's doing more than giving you permission to avoid some immediate task. It's suggesting you can live a life where you *never* have to push beyond your limits. Until her mother died, Beth had no experience of struggle. Convincing her she wasn't up to the new demands was like taking candy from a baby for Part X.

Everyone has moments when life overwhelms them and they don't feel they have the energy to fight back. You are glued to the couch, too mesmerized by the TV to get up and exercise. You allow your kids to stay up an extra hour because you don't have the energy to corral them into bed. You need to get to the office early, but you're too exhausted to get up when the alarm sounds. You feel unable to meet the demand of the moment, so you skip exercising, let the kids stay up late, or hit the snooze alarm seven times.

The following short exercise will introduce you to your own personal version of this temporary paralysis.

- Close your eyes and visualize yourself in a situation where there's something you need to do but you "just don't have the energy." The smaller, more commonplace and frequent the action, the better. Let yourself be taken over by the feeling that it's impossible to take this step.

These small moments of paralysis are more widespread than we'd like to admit. There are also those moments where you drag yourself into action without any vitality or pleasure. You have the Life Force of a zombie.

What about the things you must do no matter how lazy or depleted you are: you have to pick up the kids at a certain time; your boss sends you on a business trip on the other side of the country; you must stop at the next gas station or run out of gas in the middle of the night. Not doing these things could lead to serious consequences—you can't leave your kids waiting on a street corner for an hour. But you feel absolutely depleted, emptied of your last drop of energy. Where will you turn for the energy you need but don't have?

Walk into the nearest convenience store and the answer is staring at you from every shelf and rack—coffee, cigarettes, candy, cake, energy drinks, etc.— an endless array of artificial ways to stimulate yourself.

We're so used to this we don't even think of it as a problem. But substances make things worse. As we become tolerant of a given substance, we need to take more and more of it, often reaching the point where we need some kind of fix just to feel normal. This is classic Part X: it leads you to a problem you don't have to have (lack of energy because you've disengaged from the world) and then guides you to a solution (addictive use of substances) *that makes the problem worse.*

THE PRICE OF LOW ENERGY

The consequences of living without enough energy are huge. Shuffling through life with your flame on low makes everything difficult and some things impossible. There are the obvious losses: the places you don't go, the people you don't meet, the things you don't learn. But there are other parts of life that you wouldn't think of as requiring energy that in fact do, and when it runs out, you pay on a more fundamental level.

You lose a sense of self.

Your sense of self is the part of you that contains your goals, your values, your sense of meaning. It's the independent part of you that's the answer to the question "Who am I?" Part X constantly attacks your sense of self. It makes you doubt your potential and mistrust your instincts.

To have a strong identity you have to fend off these X attacks. That takes energy. If your energy is low you lose your identity—you float through life without direction or conviction.

You lose the ability to dream and envision your future.

The way you see the future depends on how much energy you have. People with low energy see the future in limited terms. They don't dream big, because they don't have the energy to make their dreams real. They live day to day, resigned to an endless stream of sameness. The future is created right now, but only if you have the energy to create it.

In Beth's case, she stopped working toward a future of her own, thinking she could "save" that energy and use it to survive. It was as if she took her future to the pawnshop and all she got back in return was daily admission to a lifeless present.

You miss opportunities.

What happens to you in life depends to a great extent on how you respond to opportunities. You can imagine an opportunity as a wormhole, a cosmic shortcut between the present and the future. If you reach through that passageway, you can directly influence your future.

You never know when an opportunity will present itself. Opportunities don't come in a steady, measured stream—they happen quickly and unexpectedly and they don't last forever. If you're not alert and ready to act, they will pass you by. But keeping yourself in a state of readiness takes energy.

Beth learned this the hard way. She got a message from someone whose name didn't ring a bell. Beth had catered a small party for her years ago and she wanted to hire her again. Beth let ten days pass before responding. When she did she was shocked to find the job was a major corporate function for a company now run by the client whose name she had forgotten. But the job had gone to another firm.

Beth blamed her screw-up on exhaustion but that did nothing to prepare her for the next opportunity. Only a heightened state of readiness could do that—and that required energy she didn't have.

You can't sustain relationships.

Sustaining a relationship requires more than having feelings for someone, no matter how strong they might be. Your emotions must be expressed—not just once in a while, but all the time. The word *emotion* is derived from French and Latin words meaning "to move out." An emotion isn't complete until it's expressed, or "moved out" into the world. That takes energy.

Beth didn't have the energy to "move" her loving emotions "out" to reach her husband. Her inability to connect to him left him feeling abandoned. When he demanded more time and attention, she withdrew further, leaving him feeling even more lonely. They were caught in a cycle that kept building on itself.

Beth wanted to believe it was all her husband's fault: "No matter how much I give, it's never enough." But her own depleted state set this cycle in motion; until she had the energy to correct it they were on a merry-go-round with no way to get off.

THE LIE THAT KEEPS US EXHAUSTED

Beth and Eileen were both full of life as teenagers. Yet, as adults, Eileen was still bursting with energy while Beth hovered on the verge of exhaustion. Beth's explanation for this was telling: "You only get so much energy. Eileen was born with more than I was. Mine got used up first." That attitude lay at the core of her problem.

Beth, like most people, thought of life energy as a fixed trait like blood type or eye color. We are born with a certain amount of energy and *there's nothing we can do to change that*. This is the lie that kept Beth from reenergizing herself. It's a lie we believe so deeply it's never challenged, least of all by psychiatrists.

When a psychiatrist gets a new patient, the first thing they want to know is the diagnosis—what's wrong with this person? The first thing *I* want to know is what resources the patient already has—what's right with this person? Their most important resource is their energy level. Those with the highest energy are most likely to succeed, no matter what the diagnosis. Even for those not in therapy, the best predictor of future potential—how far they'll go in life—is how much energy they have.

What about those without a lot of energy? They deserve help too. When I first meet them they're typically in some stage of withdrawl from the world, fearful their energy will run out altogether. Their goal isn't to grow, it's to survive. In Beth's words, "Once that energy gets used, I'm up the creek without a paddle."

As long as she believed there was no remedy for her exhaustion, it became a self-fulfilling prophecy. But there was a much better way for Beth to understand why she had so little energy.

Eileen had more energy than Beth because Eileen remained engaged with the world, even in the worst of times. To be engaged is to fully immerse yourself in life rather than just going through the motions.

Engagement is an ongoing process, a way of being. No one action—even if dramatic—makes you engaged.

Engagement isn't something that happens to you; it means reaching out to the world on your own initative.

Engagement doesn't have to involve "important" actions; only actions that are meaningful to you.

When engaged with the world you feel more alive; and with that awakened Life Force comes energy. Where does this energy come from? From inside you; specifically, from your body. This "energy of engagement" is stimulated by the demands of the world around you. You need physical energy to engage, but once you do your body responds by creating more energy. You can use this newly created energy to engage further. For many people this is a self-sustaining cycle: if energy was an investment we'd say it offers a great return. But you have to be able to make the initial deposit.

You want to re-engage in as many areas of life as you can. In Beth's case that would include maintaining more friendships, a greater commitment to her business, more time and interest in family activities, finding physical activities she enjoyed.

To give you a concrete picture of what re-engagement looks like, here are some of the things I told Beth to do.

Be present and active at the events she catered

Reconnect to her friends

Carve out time dedicated to her family

Find a physical activity that had some pleasure in it

Rest without complete withdrawal from her life; a twenty-minute nap, not a two-hour escape

I told Beth she'd have no relationship with her daughter until she made these changes—she wouldn't have the energy. She looked at me like I'd asked her to climb Mount Everest.

"That's easy for you to say. Starting to make all these changes takes energy—and I just don't have any."

Beth was up against The Paradox of Engagement. To generate new energy, you must engage with the world. But you can't engage with the world without energy. It's similar to borrowing money from a bank: they'll only lend it to you if you already have money.

PHYSICAL VERSUS SPIRITUAL ENERGY

Everyone faces this issue at some point. Even if you normally have plenty of energy, sooner or later you'll find yourself in a situation that overwhelms you and leaves you depleted. You want to re-engage with life, but, like a boxer who just got knocked down, you can't find the energy to get up off the mat.

Whether your depletion is temporary or long-standing you face the same paradox: how can you buy into this energy system when you don't have enough energy to make the initial deposit? You can't. *But what if there was another kind of energy* that doesn't come from your body, energy you could access with very little effort? If the energy of engagement is physical, we would describe this other kind of energy as spiritual.

Calling it "spiritual energy" doesn't imply it's linked to organized religion or a mystical belief system. We call it spiritual because its source isn't your physical body or anything else in the material world we live in.

You can run out of physical energy—that's what exhaustion is. But spiritual energy is limitless—available even when you are physically depleted. It's the solution to the Paradox of Engagement—ensuring you'll always have enough energy to engage with the world.

The diagram below depicts the inevitable diminishment of physical energy and how spiritual energy compensates for that loss.

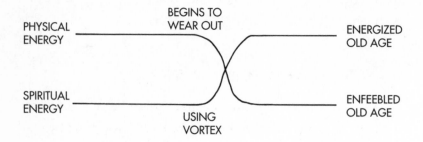

The line beginning at the top left represents the level of physical energy a person has at a given age. This energy is purely biological—its source is your body. It is responsible for the tremendous vitality of children and young adults. Because it's physical, it diminishes over time, which is why the the line slopes downward as it moves to the right. The reduction in physical energy this represents causes the changes associated with getting older: fatigue, stiff joints, weak muscles, and so on.

The inevitable loss of physical energy is viewed as a weakness by society. Patients in their mid-fifties and older often complain about feeling shunted aside. Their younger peers don't value the wisdom they've gained through years of experience. It's as if their lives have amounted to nothing.

The only antidote is to systematically increase your spiritual energy. You've probably met an older person who still has enthusiasm for life. You can see it in the way their eyes twinkle and hear it in the way they laugh. They are tapped into a higher energy. Their age is irrelevant—the world takes them seriously because they're fully alive. There are rare individuals who do this naturally; the rest of us need to use a tool.

The line starting at the lower left represents this spiritual energy. It doesn't come from your body but from a realm infinitely larger than any individual. You don't create this energy, you access it.

As powerful as spiritual energy is, my patients had a hard time believing it existed. Appealing to their intellect was useless. Only by feeling the presence of this energy for themselves could they accept its reality.

There is a part of each of us that can directly experience non-material energy. We've been calling it the soul. Others call it the spirit or the Higher Self. Sometimes a patient will say they've always thought of themselves as energy.

It's not important what you call it, what matters is knowing how to use it to tap into the boundless reserves of non-physical energy that are always within reach. The Vortex is the tool that allows you to do that.

THE TOOL: THE VORTEX

The Vortex combines two age-old symbols in a new way: the Sun and the number twelve. The Sun represents the endless source of spiritual energy. Twelve is traditionally the number of completeness—there are twelve months in the year, twelve signs in the Zodiac, and twelve hours on a clock face.

You can put these two symbols together by imagining a

circle of twelve suns. This symbolizes the totality of all the spiritual energy in the universe; the circle represents this energy functioning as one focused whole.

To share in this overflowing energy, you need a way to rise through the circle of suns. What makes this possible is a vortex—a swirling force shaped like a tornado but without a tornado's destructive power.

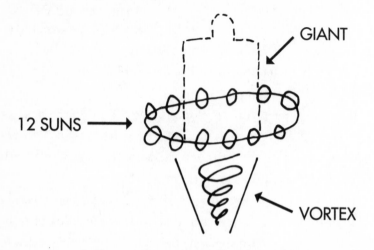

THE VORTEX

TWELVE SUNS: See twelve suns in a circle lined up directly over your head. Summon the Vortex by silently screaming the word "help" at them with focused intensity. This will set the entire circle of suns spinning, creating a gentle tornado-shaped vortex.

RISE: Relax and allow your body to become one with the vortex. Feel the pull of the vortex as it lifts you up through the circle of suns.

GROW: Once you're through the circle, feel yourself grow into a giant with unlimited energy, moving slowly but deliberately through the world without any resistance.

In using this tool, the only time you need to make a physical effort is at the moment you scream "help" to summon the Vortex. It need only last for a second—stay relaxed for the rest of the tool.

When you're exhausted, your body feels dense and heavy, like something you drag along with you. When you relax and dissolve into the vortex, your body loses its heaviness. With no further effort you grow into a giant, carried forward by the Life Force. In this state, you feel infinitely expansive.

Physical energy is focused on some "thing" you want to acquire—money, a spouse, revenge, a nice car, an Ivy League education. Like a lab rat who can't stop pushing a lever to get a reward, you pursue what you're attached to until you have no energy left.

Spiritual energy isn't driven to any kind of victory or success in the outside world. It's without the grasping, win-or-lose quality of physical energy. It's unexpectedly slow and gentle, yet it's unstoppable.

When you use the Vortex, you do more than reenergize yourself—you put yourself in sync with the higher world. As long as you stay in harmony with this spiritual energy, you'll move forward in life with a sense of ease you've never felt before.

Infinity is unhurried. It moves and creates with a slow, gentle calmness. To access the infinite, you have to move the same way it does. That's a problem for most people—they lack the patience. Like a child who wants dessert before he has finished his vegetables, the ego wants its gratification now.

That attitude won't get you to your goal any faster. In fact, it slows you down because it destroys the harmony between you and the infinite. If you insist on marching to the beat of your own drum, you'll end up in a one-person orchestra.

How and When to Use the Vortex

There are two different kinds of situations where you benefit hugely from using the Vortex.

The first are those times when you don't have the energy to engage with the world. There are a variety of causes, but they all leave you in the same condition: stuck. There's nothing subtle about these situations—you are fully aware there is no gas left in your tank.

You need extra energy to get life going again, but you have no idea where to get it from. Part X tells you not to even try, that it's *impossible* to change your basic energy level. Once you believe that initial lie, a sense of impossibility spreads through your being, as if Part X whispered its own mantra, "You can't do it."

But you can. You have access to an endless reservoir of energy. Its presence refutes the lie of impossibility—but you must *feel* its presence, not just read about it. That means using the Vortex and feeling the gentle, unhurried power it creates.

Use the tool when you've disengaged from life and can't find the energy to put yourself back into forward motion. Below are descriptions of the three most common ways lack of energy manifests itself.

Paralysis

The most obvious time to use the Vortex is in those moments when you're paralyzed by exhaustion. Your physical body feels too heavy to move, and it seems impossible to get up off the couch or out of bed. You feel used up, your energy stores depleted. This is the situation Beth was in.

Don't try to force yourself back into action. Use the Vortex a few times *without moving*. All you want to do is become aware of the gently flowing energy above the ring of suns. Do it a few more times and then begin to move gently and slowly, staying in harmony with the spiritual energy.

Spacing Out

"Spacing out" is another condition in which you're unable to find the energy to move forward. When you're paralyzed, your body feels too heavy to move; when you're spaced out, you've lost your connection to your body altogether. For minutes, even hours, you drift without a sense of direction, in your own world. You might find yourself slumped in front of the TV, not knowing what you're watching, or letting your mind wander during a conversation, not hearing a word that was said.

Spacing out is a *lack of concentration*, and it takes energy to bring things back into focus. Use the Vortex a few times and focus the higher energy you generate not on doing anything, but on bringing your attention back to the present. Once you feel your focus returning, you can use the tool a few more times to energize a physical action.

Feeling Overwhelmed

We all have times when life floods us with an overwhelming number of demands. You haven't paid your water bill, you've left the clothing you need at the cleaners, your child is waiting to be picked up at school, you just got a parking ticket—and on top of all of that you're having guests for dinner and the house is a mess.

Our first reaction to this onslaught is to speed up, trying to get everything done at once. This leads to a frenzy of multitasking, aided and abetted by the smartphone. It seems like you're getting a lot done, but you end up running around like a chicken without a head.

You can't move forward when you're panicked and directionless. Forward motion needs the calm, deliberate force of spiritual energy. Hyperactivity and its evil stepchild, multitasking, make it impossible to connect with this pleasant, measured energy.

Each time you feel pulled into hyperactivity, especially if you're tempted to multitask, use the Vortex. Repeat the tool several times if necessary. Get into the habit of connecting to its calm, focused energy the moment you begin to feel overwhelmed.

Transitions

The previous examples described situations in which you are unable to move forward in life. Whether you're paralyzed, spaced out, or hyperactive, the underlying problem is a lack of energy. There's no mystery about this—you know there is an energy deficit even if you don't know how to correct it.

There's a second kind of energy shortage that isn't as obvious. It acts like an invisible force pushing back against you, actively resisting each step you take. Because you feel its resistance all day, every day, you don't see its presence as a problem—it's "just the way things are." It doesn't stop your forward motion, but it makes every step a fight.

All of us are caught in an invisible war between forces that push us back and those that move us forward. This war isn't fought in a few climactic battles; it's fought in small skirmishes that come a thousand times a day. A skirmish occurs every time life makes a demand on us. The demands are small but they never stop coming.

You get out of bed in the morning, wake up the kids, start breakfast, check email and social media, wash and dress yourself, etc. These small demands continue until, exhausted, you fall into bed at night. Each of these tasks doesn't require much energy in and of itself. What's draining is the effort required to repeatedly *move from one event to the next*. We call this shift of effort and attention to the next task a "transition."

Why are transitions so difficult? In high school science, we were all taught Newton's first law of motion: a body at rest stays at rest, a body in motion stays in motion. This tendency is called inertia. As human beings, we're subject to our own form of inertia: it's easier to keep doing what we're already doing than to move to a new task.

Ask yourself the following: Can you get up and walk away when your favorite TV show ends? Can you end a conversation with someone and make a phone call you've been putting off? Can you tear yourself away from Facebook to start making dinner?

Not so easy. You may not have that extra bit of energy you need to transition into the next step. But life is movement, and, ready or not, here comes the next demand. No matter how trivial the task—brushing your teeth, gassing up your car—if you just sit there, making an excuse for inaction, you've fallen out of sync with the universe and the spiritual forces it can give you. This inability to make transitions is the secret cause of much of the dissatisfaction and fatigue that plague us. It makes life feel like an uphill slog.

This creates another use for the Vortex, maybe its most important use: the tool gives you the energy to overcome your inertia and to keep moving through the endless transitions life demands. Most people focus on the bigger, more challenging events in life, but the forces that drive the universe function on a much smaller level. We call this the world of small things—"things" in the sense of minor, seemingly inconsequential acts. Just the way modern physics studies matter at the level of the smallest particles, the best way to understand human behavior is at the level of the most common actions and events.

Rudolf Steiner, the great European philosopher, put it this way: *the most important things* enter the world through the *smallest things*. The commonplace is crucial because most of our time is spent doing commonplace things. What matters is the ability to keep moving through everyday transitions: you leave work, pick up your dry cleaning, go home, and hang it in the closet. Not exactly a hero's journey, but your ability to make these transitions keeps you in endless movement—and this state of endless motion makes you a container for the higher forces that allow you to reach your full potential.

As Pablo Picasso said, "Inspiration exists, but it has to find you working." What does he mean by "working"? As a painter and sculptor, he was alluding to the creative process of an artist, but anyone who's creating anything—a business, a family, a building—is subject to the same kind of process.

For a writer, "work" involves showing up at the computer each morning for the daily struggle of writing. Just the act of showing up means you've fought your way through a transition. But that's not enough. During the writing session, there will be times you'll feel blocked, distracted, or demoralized. Part of the "work" is to transition back into the flow of the writing. Using the Vortex at those moments gives you the strength to keep going.

This focus on "just keep going" is more important than how good or bad the writing is—your opinions about quality are irrelevant. As long as you keep writing, you're doing the work of creating. You can't know when inspiration will come, but as long as you keep working, whenever it does you'll be there to receive it.

It takes faith to commit yourself to this kind of process, faith that your efforts will eventually be rewarded. Part X will mock you for being willing to work this hard with no guarantees. You can't dispel its lies with words. The only thing that will help is to use the Vortex at those moments. The energy you create *is* your assertion that you won't be stopped.

The Rewards of Using the Vortex

It takes time to experience the full power of the Vortex, but if you let the cues trigger your use of the tool, you'll receive an immediate reward—more energy. That will lead you to a humbling discovery: your view of the future isn't the product of careful planning and preparation; it's the result of how much energy you have. *Optimism is the sensation of overflowing energy that never gets used up.*

When I suggested that Beth use the tool to restore her lack of energy, she was understandably skeptical. "It's just one more thing I don't have the energy to do." I told her to start with something small, maybe an unpleasant phone call she didn't have the strength to make. At first she objected, saying, "I came here because my daughter won't talk to me. What does that have to do with phone calls?"

She soon found out. She came to the next session excited and confused at the same time. "It worked. I used the tool and it definitely gave me more energy, so I made the call. I thought it was impossible that a tool could help." But that wasn't all. "The next day, I made two more calls I hadn't even planned on, hard calls, to people who owed me money. I was getting better at the tool, so when I got home I really went for it . . . I played with my daughter, and she let me."

"That's a great first step."

"What do you mean, 'first step'? I did the Vortex every

day before I played with her. I even did it *while* I was playing with her."

"What did you do when you were finished playing?"

"Well, I went to my room, shut the phone off, and went to sleep for an hour. I always have to get in my nap."

"Were you tired?"

"No . . . in fact I couldn't sleep, but I never know when my energy will run out, so I try to store some up."

I reminded Beth she couldn't hoard energy like a squirrel socking away nuts for the winter. Access to nonstop energy comes when you use the Vortex to power your engagement with the world. You don't *have* this new energy; you create it every moment.

Beth had been disengaged from the world for so long she needed a blueprint to reconnect. Her plan needed to include ways to reconnect in each of the major life areas from which she had withdrawn.

At work, she needed to actively reach out to her existing customers and market to new customers.

In her marriage, she needed to be proactive in rebuilding her sexual and emotional connection to her husband.

She needed to restart old friendships and make an effort to start new ones.

For herself, she needed to find something new—creative, intellectual, or spiritual—that was meaningful to her.

She needed a physical outlet—not just working out in the gym—she could find some passion for.

When I laid all this out for Beth, she was overwhelmed. She'd lived for years putting little energy into these major life areas. She was leery of taking on too much and "using up" whatever energy she still had. Part X encouraged this limited view of herself.

But because she didn't want to lose the relationship with her daughter, she kept using the Vortex to energize anything she did with her. If she couldn't bring herself to tackle any other areas of life, at least she had that. She told herself it was a pretty good deal.

But it was really a deal with the devil. You can't bargain with higher forces. Either you're committed to engaging in life as a whole or you lose your energy and vitality—and, in Beth's case, your relationship with your daughter.

Weeks went by. In every session, I harped on the need for Beth to spread her wings and engage in a full life. She resisted the message until the one person who could convince her spoke—her daughter.

Beth had just picked her daughter up from a playdate. The moment she got in the car, Beth felt a tension that hadn't been there when she'd dropped her off. Beth immediately asked, "What's the matter?"

"Sarah's mom had these other moms over and they were going to a play. Why don't you have any friends or ever do anything like that?" her daughter asked.

Beth's heart dropped to her stomach. She knew instantly the question was about much more than friends. Her daughter was asking her why she didn't have a life of her own. This bothered her more than she expected. Up to that point, she'd used the tool to get through specific situations and then crawl back into her withdrawn shell. But now her daughter was asking of her what she should have been asking of herself: real commitment to life.

That would demand more than a few phone calls or even playing with her daughter. It meant re-engaging with the world in every area of her life—including her work, marriage, friends, and physical health. It was that realization that made her heart drop; she was afraid she didn't have the energy. I explained that X wanted her to believe that her energy was too low to make efforts in all these areas; it had been brainwashing her with this lie since her mother died.

But things had changed; after using the tool for a little while, she was now closer to her daughter than she'd been before. When Beth got lazy or withdrawn, she saw her failure reflected in the disappointment on her daughter's face. Every time her daughter reacted this way, Beth was motivated to work harder to take back her life. Sometimes she succeeded, sometimes she failed, but once she realized her relationship with her daughter was dependent on how fully alive she could be, Beth determined never to give up.

FREQUENTLY ASKED QUESTIONS

I used the Vortex, and I could feel myself getting bigger, but I didn't feel any more energy. Am I doing it wrong?

No, you're not doing it wrong. Some people are so used to their body being their sole source of energy that when they feel spiritual energy for the first time, it doesn't feel like "energy" to them. Our society equates energy with a loud, heart-pounding, adrenaline-infused caffeine rush. Spiritual energy is subtler than that; it's quiet, undramatic, and steady. It hums at a lower (but longer-lasting) frequency. It's a peaceful calmness that goes on forever. As you get used to the tool, you'll feel the gentle but unstoppable power of this higher kind of energy.

When I use the tool, I get the most energy when I keep my feet on the ground as the vortex lifts my body through the circle of twelve suns. I feel huge and elongated, amazed at how big I've become. Is this okay?

Yes, you're not alone in using the tool this way. The first time I encountered someone using the Vortex like this was with Barry Michels, who constantly works to make every tool more effective. Focusing on your feet does two good things. First, it directs the energy the tool generates down to the everyday material world where you can use it to solve real problems. Second, when you look down and see how far away your feet are, you magnify the sense that you have assumed the size and power of a giant.

Can you use the Vortex in situations that aren't personal but still feel overwhelming, such as acts of terrorism, natural disasters, or economic or political crises?

Yes. The key to dealing with catastrophic events is to remain engaged with the world. This gives you access to the help and information that you need. A catastrophe changes your perception of what the world is, but if you have any leadership responsibilities, including parenting, it's particularly crucial not to withdraw. An explosion in a public place, an earthquake, or a stock market crash destroys the sense of predictability and familiarity that make us feel safe. When we're confused and terrified, paralysis often sets in.

One of the greatest spiritual and practical skills you can develop is the ability to take action in a crisis while remaining calm. The calm but unstoppable energy the Vortex produces is perfectly suited for staying engaged with a world that has become uncertain. After 9/11, one of my patients, the CEO of a huge company with thousands of employees, became so paralyzed he didn't go to work for several days. Using the Vortex allowed him to return to his job and its responsibilities, assuaging the fears of his employees. It also made him confident that he could deal with the unexpected in whatever future form it might take.

How do I know if I need rest or if I'm just being lazy?

The best way to make that distinction is to look at the context. Resting—whether it's taking a nap, watching something on TV, reading, or allowing yourself any other form of downtime—will look and feel different depending on your goals. If your goal is to live in constant forward motion, then you rest to restore the energy you need to take the next step in life. You end up feeling relaxed and rejuvenated.

If you're not in forward motion, you rest to *escape* from the world. This is rest as immediate gratification; it's not preparation for the next step because there is no next step. It leaves you with less energy than when you started. This drive to withdraw from the world is what causes a two-hour nap when twenty minutes would be sufficient.

A person committed to forward motion knows, *before they start their nap*, what they're going to do when they wake up. They also have a pretty accurate sense of how long they want to rest. When they awake, they are eager to take the next action. The person without a sense of forward motion, without goals or the sense of a next step, has no idea what they'll be doing when they wake up. That's the definition of laziness: rest for its own sake, without a purpose or an end point.

OTHER USES OF THE VORTEX

THE VORTEX GIVES YOU THE ENERGY TO STAND UP FOR YOURSELF. A HUGE NUMBER OF PEOPLE DON'T LIVE THE LIFE THEY WANT. They live the life they're pushed into by other people, like a boss, a parent, a spouse, or even a friend. When others are demanding, bullying, insistent, or just plain selfish, and you don't have the strength to push back and say no, your passivity makes you feel small and childlike. The Vortex reverses this; it brings a sense of increased size and power that makes you feel like an adult who can stand up for himself.

José was the only child of a single mother. As a child, he saw himself as her protector, and by the time he was sixteen he assumed that role in reality. His mother took advantage of this. She took most of what he earned at his part-time job. In the little time José had outside of work and school, she expected him to do errands for her, drive her to appointments, and make their meals. But no matter how much he did, it was never enough. She complained constantly, keeping him in a state of perpetual guilt. When he wasn't at her beck and call—which happened more frequently as he got older—she would fly into a rage.

When he was twenty-eight, he opened a convenience store. It was an immediate success, but it took up most of his time. His only personal time was Sunday afternoon; he was willing to spend it with his mother except during the football season, when he watched the games with his friends. His relationship with his mother reached a turning point when she called him during a big game and insisted he come over to her house immediately. When he found himself involuntarily getting his car keys, he realized she could still make him feel like an intimidated child. No longer willing to live his life for someone else, he began to use the Vortex. Within a few weeks, he felt "bigger" and more adult. From this new perspective, it became obvious his mother's bark was worse than her bite. Standing up to her became much easier as long as he kept using the tool.

THE VORTEX GIVES YOU THE COURAGE TO DO THINGS YOU NEVER THOUGHT WERE POSSIBLE. Most of us go through life burdened with a sense of extreme limitation. We do the same things, have the same interests, even think the same thoughts. These habits keep us in a familiar, seemingly safe world, created and maintained by Part X. To find yourself, to satisfy yourself, you have to move beyond the limited world Part X created. This isn't a matter of thinking, it's a matter of *action*. Using the Vortex gives you the courage to take risks and act even when the outcome is uncertain. It's your way into a world of possibilities that Part X doesn't want you to know exists.

Roy was raised by two loving but fearful parents. They didn't savor life, they survived it. In a murky corner of their minds, an unpredictable catastrophe was always about to happen. They tried to protect themselves by living as timidly as possible. They both held safe, boring, lifelong civil service jobs, counting the weeks and months until they could collect their pensions. With the best of intentions, they insisted that Roy live the same kind of risk-free life they did, subject to the same limitations.

Roy wanted something more from life than that, but by this time he was in his late twenties, with a mortgage, a wife, and a child. His parents made him feel this was such a crushing responsibility that he had no choice but to take the same kind of safe job they had. From his first week on the job as a program manager for the state, he knew it was a mistake. When he thought of being trapped in this situation for thirty years, it felt like a prison sentence. His parents reassured him he'd adjust to the job and would grow to appreciate its security. He knew they were wrong, but because of the fear of the future they'd instilled in him he felt paralyzed, unable to see any alternatives.

He was sinking into a gray funk when a close friend with an entrepreneurial bent revealed he had raised the money for a tech start-up and wanted Roy to become his partner. It was an exciting offer in an area Roy was interested in. But it was a risk—a leap off a cliff unlike anything he'd ever done before.

To his surprise, his wife supported the idea. She encouraged him to go for it, telling him if he didn't try, he'd regret it for the rest of his life. Her reaction left him without any excuse—he knew he had to act. After Roy used the Vortex for several weeks, he found an instinctive courage that freed him to imagine the possibilities of a different life than the one he felt stuck in.

THE VORTEX HELPS YOU MOVE PAST CREATIVE BLOCKS. What makes us distinct from every other being in the universe is our ability to find creative solutions to our problems. There are, however, times when the creative process seems to abandon us. This happens to everyone—from a novelist to a parent to a small business owner to a salesperson to a high school athlete. These are moments when your mind suddenly goes blank: a writer might say they are "blocked"; a performer would say they "froze." These are versions of the same experience: the flow of ideas and insights that make up the creative process shuts down. This is the

> work of Part X. It subjects your ideas and instincts to
> such harsh judgments that you lose all confidence. It
> doesn't matter whether you are judging yourself or
> imagine others are judging you. Words can't free
> you from this state; you need energy. This means
> using the Vortex—its infinite, creative power can
> overcome any blocks Part X puts in your way.

Marta was a serious student of philosophy and spirituality. This was her great passion. A deep thinker, she had many
provocative ideas. But when she thought about expressing
them to others, either in writing or out loud, Part X would
attack, telling her that her ideas were silly and that if she put
them out there she would make a fool of herself. Because of
this, she kept her ideas to herself, and others had no idea how
deep and original her thinking was.

She'd been attending a community church for many years.
One Sunday a month, a member of the church was invited to
give the sermon. Marta had declined the invitation several
times. One Wednesday morning, the preacher called her and
asked for a favor. He was going to be out of town and the
guest speaker for that Sunday had just backed out. He wanted
to know if Marta would give the sermon. She felt a familiar
fear at the thought of organizing her ideas and presenting
them with the passion she felt, but with his encouragement
decided to accept the challenge.

The moment she sat down to write, her worst fears were
realized. Instead of coming up with her normal, prolific flow
of thoughts, her mind went blank. It felt impossible for her to
access the creative, impassioned state she was used to—it

was as if she had lost connection to a part of herself. She was able to restore that connection using the Vortex. It gave her the energy to reconnect to her Life Force and fight her way through whatever blocks Part X put in her way. It also gave her the confidence she needed to get up in front of the congregation and deliver her sermon.

SUMMARY

HOW PART X ATTACKS YOU: *It overwhelms and exhausts you, making it seem as if the only way to preserve your energy is to stop trying to meet life's demands.*

HOW THIS DEADENS YOU: *Life energy comes from meeting, not disengaging from, the demands of life. The more Part X gets you to withdraw, the less energy you have, and the more you convince yourself of the need to withdraw further. Rather than expanding, your life contracts.*

HOW PART X TRICKS YOU INTO GIVING IN: *It convinces you that your energy is finite, so that when you feel depleted, you don't try to look for other sources of energy. Depletion becomes an end point, like a death.*

THE SOLUTION: *The Vortex enables you to tap into an infinite source of energy, giving you the power to continue meeting life's demands, even when you feel you can't.*

Chapter Five

The Tool: The Mother

Barry shows you how to build your resilience so you can get back up no matter how many times life knocks you down. The Mother tool gives you a sense of optimism that sustains you through setbacks and defeats; it enables you to pursue your dreams.

Ann, an attractive thirty-something, trudged into my office and sank into the couch. Her face was pale and she was clearly struggling with her emotions. I asked her what was wrong.

She rolled her eyes and reached for a tissue. "I told myself I wasn't going to cry, but I can't seem to stop."

"Did something happen?"

"Another relationship bit the dust. It's happened a million times—you'd think I'd be used to it by now," she said, attempting a smile.

"Has every breakup gotten to you this much?"

"No." She struggled to hold back the tears. "I've always

been able to pull myself together within a few weeks. But I don't feel like I'm ever going to get over this one. It's the best relationship I've ever been in, and we both walked away from it."

As we talked, it became clear that Ann only felt fully alive when she was in a relationship—without one, life felt color-less and empty. "All I've ever wanted, really, was to find the right guy and be loved by him."

I asked her how far back the search for love went. She thought for a moment. "I guess it started with my dad." It turned out their entire relationship was a series of failed at-tempts by Ann to get her father to pay attention to her. A handsome, charismatic figure, he held court every night in the neighborhood bar, regaling his friends with endless sto-ries. "I had the shitty job of ending the party and dragging him home. I kept thinking he'd be happy to see me, but he never was. He'd lift his beer mug and greet me with a joke, like 'Honey, there's an empty swimming pool right down the block. Why don't you go practice your diving?' His buddies would roar with laughter. On the way home, I'd be crying, but he never noticed."

Sometimes Ann felt so dejected she'd fall into a black hole, moping in her room and refusing to speak to anyone. She got out of it the only way she knew: with fantasy. "I imagined him taking me out to a special dinner, looking into my eyes, and really showing interest in me." The fantasy spurred her on to greater efforts. She'd try to impress him with her knowledge of football, greet him at the door with his favorite drink, and laugh the loudest at his jokes.

This never worked, but the pattern continued after she

left home. With a generous, big-hearted disposition, she would do almost anything to get men to love her. One of her first serious relationships was with a wannabe musician. When he complained that his day job didn't leave him enough time to write songs, she took two jobs and supported both of them. Her boyfriend used his newfound free time to sleep with as many women as possible. "When I confronted him, he said it was my fault, that I was spending too much time at work. Then he dumped me."

Anne was naïve, but she wasn't weak. When a relationship ended, she'd feel despondent for a while. Then she'd pick herself up and vow to pursue someone better. That's exactly what happened with the musician. "Looking back, I realized his goal was to get a free ride—he wouldn't even pay for groceries. That's when I decided never to date anyone who couldn't pay his own way. I immediately felt better."

After that, whoever she dated supported himself. But life turned out to be more complicated than she'd anticipated. She went through a series of guys who were so independent they had no desire to be part of her life. "One guy would take me to the most expensive restaurants in the city, but he wouldn't set foot in my apartment. I introduced him to my best friend three times and he couldn't be bothered to remember her name. I was patient, hoping he'd eventually take down the wall. Instead, he broke up with me."

"Did that hopeless feeling come back?"

"Yeah. For a while, all I could do was mope around, watch chick flicks, and whine to my friends. But then I realized that the last guy had been a big improvement on the slacker musician. I hadn't struck gold yet, but it felt like I was getting closer."

Then she met Luke, and he quickly became her primary focus. He seemed to have everything: ambitious and successful, he also genuinely wanted to be part of her life. "We spent every night together. He wanted to meet my friends—he even remembered all their names. It was a magical time. Every day felt new and exciting."

But gradually, the thrill subsided. "After a while, I started to feel let down, like 'This isn't nearly as good as I thought it was going to be.' I remember sitting at my desk, planning to see him after work, and realizing he didn't seem special anymore. I could've been going out with anyone."

It only got worse from there. Little things about him began to irritate her—his smell, the noises he made when he ate. When he hugged her, she wanted to squirm away. "It kept going downhill, and I didn't know how to stop it. He sensed something was wrong, and when I told him the truth, he said the magic had faded for him too. So we called it quits." She started to tear up again. "I always thought it was just a matter of finding the right guy. But I finally found him and it *still* didn't work out. Now it's clear: I'm going to be alone for the rest of my life."

THE PROBLEM: FALSE HOPE

Ann felt hopeless, and I sympathized with her pain. But I also thought that the breakup was the best thing that could've happened to her. When I told her this, I could see her wanting to believe me. But the sense of defeat and loss was too crushing. "I reject the first man who's ever truly loved me, and you're telling me it's the best thing that's ever happened?"

"It's the only way you could accept the truth: you were looking for more than a relationship—you were looking for magic. You can get a sense of it right now. Close your eyes and go back to that moment you realized Luke was a disappointment. What was missing?"

"I wanted life to feel as exciting as it did when I first met him."

That was the perfect answer—perfect for revealing Ann's problem. She wanted more from Luke than a loving relationship. She was looking for a magical solution to all the dark feelings every person has to deal with from time to time. She wanted Luke to keep her life inspiring and stimulating, to spare her from boredom and loneliness. In essence, Ann wanted to live in the last scene of a romantic movie, where the music swells and the heroine walks off into the sunset, hand in hand with the ideal partner. And she wanted that moment to last forever.

In real life, that perfect moment is just a moment—it can't last. The heroine will have disappointments and dark times for the rest of her life. She can overcome them, but she'll have to work at it. The best relationship in the world won't do it for her.

Ann was smart, and she knew all this on a conscious level. Yet the fact that she'd spent her whole life searching for the "right guy" revealed that Part X was controlling her from the recesses of her unconscious. To Part X, the "right guy" didn't mean someone who wanted to share her life with her. It meant someone who had the power to save her from her own struggles. That person doesn't exist for anyone.

Why would Part X encourage Ann to spend her life chasing a mirage? Because that futile search could only end in one of two ways, both of them miserable. Either she'd live a life of endless yearning, never finding the kind of love she craved, or she'd get what she wanted and it wouldn't change anything. Inside, she'd still be the same unhappy person. The latter was what had happened with Luke.

You have to give the devil his due. It's a brilliant plan. But fortunately, it had one flaw, and it was the reason I told Ann the breakup was the best thing that could've happened. As crushing as it was for Ann to discover that even the "right guy" couldn't rescue her from dark moments, it was far better than wasting her life searching for and never finding a pot of gold at the end of a rainbow. Now she could stop searching for an impossible dream and learn how to make herself happy.

THE ALLURE OF FALSE HOPE

It's human nature to hope for a magical someone or something that will relieve you of the effort it takes to create happiness for yourself. Part X takes advantage of this human laziness. It takes whatever you consciously hope for—a good relationship, successful children, or a lucrative career—and converts it into an unconscious hope for magic. Then, when you don't get what you'd hoped for, Part X floods you with a crushing sense of hopelessness.

There's a name for this magical wish: false hope. You're not aware of your false hopes; they're buried in your unconscious like a hidden virus. You only discover them when you get whatever you were consciously hoping for and end up feeling let down and demoralized.

As therapists, we see these outsized reactions all the time. An entrepreneur earns millions of dollars, yet nine months later he feels like everything he's doing is meaningless. A student graduates from a top school with high honors and within a short time feels directionless. A woman with fertility problems goes from doctor to doctor until she finally gets pregnant, but after the birth she lapses into postpartum depression. What all these people have in common is that they unconsciously hoped for a one-way ticket to happiness and instead ended up with a one-way ticket to misery.

The kind of misery you suffer when your false hopes are crushed is unique. It isn't just sadness or disappointment, it's an all-pervading darkness that smothers every part of your life, a deep hole that feels impossible to climb out of.

You've felt this way at some point in your life. Everyone has. But strangely, we tend to forget how bad it was once we recover from it. Part X does that intentionally: if it can erase your memory of past holes, you're more likely to fall into future ones. We want to remind you of what the experience feels like so you'll be prepared to climb out more quickly next time. That's what this next exercise is for. Read it through completely first; once you feel you know what to do, close your eyes and try it:

- Choose a time when something you really wanted didn't work out and you felt demoralized and hopeless. It might have been the loss of someone you loved, an opportunity you were counting on that fell through, or any other kind of defeat.
- Re-create the memory as vividly as you can, as if it's happening right now. Study how you're feeling inside. In particular, has this setback changed how you feel about attaining what you want in the future?

When you fall into a hole, one of the first things it affects is your attitude about the future. You become certain you'll never get what you want. That's why Ann was so sure she'd be alone for the rest of her life. This isn't an accident. By shutting down all hope for the future, Part X can destroy your drive to do anything in the present. When Ann first came to see me, she'd spent an entire weekend lying in bed. Unopened mail was piling up, and she lacked the energy to return phone calls and emails. When I asked her why she wasn't taking care of these things, her answer was typical of someone who's lost faith in her future: "Why bother?"

THE PRICE: DEMORALIZATION KILLS

Like an opportunistic infection, this "Why bother?" attitude infects everything. Problems go unsolved. It becomes difficult to recognize opportunities that come your way, let alone pursue them energetically. If you're convinced your future is bleak, then nothing you do in the present is going to amount to anything anyway, so why bother doing it?

In extreme cases, this kind of pessimism, unchecked, can prove fatal. Over forty thousand people take their own lives each year in the United States alone. Part X has convinced them that the despair they're feeling has no remedy—death seems like the only escape.

In less extreme cases, Part X is satisfied with the "living death" we described in Chapters 1 and 2. Convinced you have no future, you might be able to get out of bed and go to work, but you're going through the motions. You can't be as creative or productive as you'd like to be. If this persists, you start to feel worthless. Eventually, it's even a struggle to get yourself to do the things that would normally give you pleasure. With no sense of purpose, you exist, but you're not truly alive.

But demoralization does more than destroy you from the inside. It also takes a tremendous toll on your relationships with family and friends. Many people who fall into this hole tend to withdraw, cutting themselves off because they don't want to be a "burden." This deprives them of the love, encouragement, and perspective that other people can provide. Others quickly alienate sources of support because all they talk about is how hopeless they feel, without *doing* anything about it. Either way, Part X wins by isolating them—destroying their relationships and increasing their sense of despair.

THE LIE THAT KEEPS US DEMORALIZED

Given the heavy price we pay for remaining in this dark place, you'd think we'd do whatever we could to pull ourselves out of it as quickly as possible. And yet we don't. The three remedies that help people who are depressed are (1) exercising on a consistent basis, (2) staying connected with other people (to get support and also to give it), and (3) engaging in activities that were meaningful to them before they got depressed—a hobby, creative project, educational pursuit, or whatever else used to bring them joy.

These remedies work because they get you moving again—physically and energetically. But surprisingly, most people reject them. Why? The answer is simple: if you move, you'll start to feel life stirring inside you, and Part X is the enemy of life. Once it puts you in the dark hole, its mission is to *keep* you there, in an immobilized state that mimics actual death. Go back to the last exercise and re-create the feelings of demoralization. If you stay with them long enough, you'll see—it really does start to feel as if your life has stopped moving forward.

On a conscious level, you'll think of excuses why you can't do anything: "I have no energy," "No one wants to listen to me complain," "My hobbies aren't going to amount to anything." But on an unconscious level, what's really happened is that Part X has convinced you that the shattering of your false hopes has actually killed you and there is no way to recover. In other words, you are dead, so you might as well not even try.

This is a heinous, life-destroying lie. Despair is not permanent—you *can* recover from it. Not only that, by learning to resuscitate yourself you'll find the pathway to a *more* meaningful and inspiring life. This doesn't mean that Part X will give up; it will flood you with demoralized feelings every chance it gets. But the person who learns to recover over and over again gains a new kind of confidence. It isn't based on never feeling bad again, it's based on the experience of lifting yourself out of those feelings quickly and assertively.

The first step to this new kind of confidence requires you to accept a difficult truth. When you're demoralized, you tend to blame it on whatever triggered it. That's why Ann was so fixated on her breakup with Luke. But the hard truth is this: *we despair because we are emotionally irresponsible.*

What does this mean? Let's take a look at Ann, for example. She was hardly the kind of person you'd think of as irresponsible. Normally, she was a bundle of high-energy giving. Her efforts to make her relationships work were endless. But there was one thing she never took responsibility for: her own mood. It went up when things went well with a man, and down when they went badly. Emotionally, she was like a puppet on a string.

Your primary emotional responsibility is to keep yourself in a positive state, no matter what's happening around you. Instead, most of us do what Ann did—we allow our inner state to be regulated by something outside us. Did the last sales presentation go well? Did your kid behave well today? Did someone just compliment you? Letting these things determine your mood is like building a house on sand.

To create a solid emotional foundation, you have to take control of your own mood. Most of us have no idea how to do this. Ann's reaction was typical: "Control my own mood? I can barely get out of bed in the morning."

It's not surprising Ann thought this was impossible. All her life, she'd ceded control over her emotional highs and lows. The fantasy of getting the "right" guy had been a drug, rescuing her whenever her mood dipped. But when she actually met that guy, he didn't have the effect on her she'd hoped for, so she fell to pieces. The only way Ann could save herself was to learn how to regulate her emotional life from the inside, independent of a man or anything else.

We all have the ability to do this—to generate an enthusiastic, inspired sense of life no matter what circumstances we're in. Unfortunately, we rarely discover this until failure forces us to look within.

THE MOTHER INSIDE

But what does it mean to "look within"? One of the very first guides to the inner world was Carl Jung. Roughly one hundred years ago, he studied the language of the unconscious as it emerged in dreams, art, and mythology. Jung felt that the images and stories that emerged were the product of invisible forces he called archetypes. Many of the archetypes represent inner resources you never knew you had. One of the most universal—and easiest to relate to—is the archetype of the Mother.

The archetypal Mother is the source of absolute love and support in the cosmos. She loves each of us individually and wants us to grow into our highest potential. This is easiest to understand if you look at what a human mother does for her infant. When an infant is hungry, she feeds them; when they're tired, she rocks them to sleep; when they're cold, she warms them. In essence, a human mother removes *physical* threats to her child's continued growth.

The archetypal Mother plays the same role in an adult's life, but the threats she removes aren't physical, they're emotional. What keeps most adults from growing emotionally is demoralization—we give up on ourselves and lose faith in our own future.

What makes the Mother such an invaluable resource is that she never loses faith in us; she sees the best even when we're blind to it. With her infallible optimism, she has the power to lift us back up when we get knocked down. In the previous chapter, you learned that your body is limited—it needs an infusion of energy from something beyond. In this chapter, it's your mind that needs help. When your hopes are crushed, you need an infusion of optimism from something beyond—that something is the Mother. When the writer and statesman Johann Wolfgang von Goethe wrote, "Night presses round me deep and deeper still, / And yet within me beams a radiant light," he was evoking the Mother. She restores your faith in your future, not by making promises about it, but by lifting your mood in the present.

It would be nice if this happened automatically, but it doesn't. In fact, it requires a lot of effort. That's because without your realizing it, Part X has trained you to reject the Mother's help. Behind every false hope—a relationship, a pile of money, or a child who gets into an Ivy League school—is the belief that once it's attained, you'll never have to regulate your mood; you'll never need the Mother. Unwittingly, for most of your life, you've placed your bets on attaining your false hopes instead of creating a relationship with her. That's why people feel so bereft of inner resources when their false hopes are crushed. It never occurred to them that they would need the Mother.

To accept her love, you must admit you need her, now

and for the rest of your life, no matter how well or poorly things go for you. She will never turn you down, but you must approach her as a responsible adult. That means you mustn't depend on anything outside yourself—a person, possession, or event—to keep you inspired and enthusiastic. You take full responsibility for your own mood, knowing that life will continue to challenge you. The Mother doesn't remove these challenges; she gives you an endless flow of positive energy with which to face them.

When I described the Mother to Ann, she reacted the way most patients do. "A lot of the time, I believe there's some kind of energy that's bigger than myself. But when I get this far down, I lose sight of everything and I don't even know what I believe anymore."

My answer was simple. "You don't have to believe it exists. What you have to do is use the tool and see what happens."

THE TOOL: THE MOTHER

In order to learn the proper use of this tool, you'll need to experience your problem in a completely new way. If you're demoralized, it's usually because you've arrived at a negative conclusion about yourself or your life. For Ann, it was "I'll be alone for the rest of my life." For most people, it's even broader: "I'll never succeed at anything," "I'm a loser," or "There's no point in trying."

Part X wants to make these conclusions as comprehensive as possible; the more of your life they encompass, the more depressed you'll get. For the same reason, it tries to

make them feel like incontrovertible truths. Part X is uncan-
nily gifted at imitating an omniscient god delivering a final
judgment from on high. We feel naked and defenseless, suc-
cumbing quickly to the idea that Part X has exposed the *real*
truth about us.

Logically, this makes no sense. No one can know what
they'll be able to achieve in their own life, especially before
it's over. I'm a good example. As I mentioned earlier, I
thought of myself as a failure well into my thirties. If I'd
given in to the "truth" Part X was purveying, I never would
have tried, much less succeeded in, achieving my goals.

Nonetheless, it's almost impossible to challenge these
negative conclusions logically; backed by the power of Part
X, they overwhelm rational thinking. But they can be overturned. The secret is to shift perspective, to see your problem
from the Mother's point of view. Part X's conclusions have
no credibility with her. She's not even listening. She sees
something much simpler: the negative thoughts and feelings,
regardless of their specific content, are a dark substance that
gets between you and her. They stop her from reaching you
and infusing you with optimism.

Seeing your own negativity the way she does—as a substance—is the first step to letting her back in. At first, this
may seem strange, but we want it to become second nature to
you. That's what the next exercise is for. Read it over completely before you try it.

- Re-create the sense of demoralization you felt in
  the earlier exercise. Close your eyes and listen to
  the conclusions you've come to about yourself and

your future: "I'll never get what I want out of life," "I'm a loser," etc. Feel the heaviness of these conclusions weighing you down, crushing the life out of you.

- Now forget about the conclusions and visualize the heaviness as an oppressive substance. Don't think; just take note of what the substance looks like. For most people, it appears as a heavy black sludge.

- Whatever it looks like, think of that substance as standing in the way of your ability to move forward. Sense how it makes recovery seem impossible.

When I took Ann through this exercise, she was surprised by what happened. "I saw the black stuff right away. It made me feel a little better. I suddenly realized it was a separate thing from me."

We've seen patient after patient have the same reaction. By coming to a negative conclusion and repeating it over and over again, you're actually holding on to it, keeping it inside you. But everything changes when you see it as a substance. Now the thoughts and feelings are no longer taking root inside your head. There's distance between you and the substance, and it has less power over you.

Now you're ready for the next step. The Mother's deepest wish is to remove this dark, poisonous sludge from your system. You can enable that to happen and free yourself from demoralization with the tool you're about to learn. But first you have to visualize the Mother in your mind's eye.

The Mother appears differently to each person, so don't

feel that there's a "right" way to see her. There are a few guidelines that will help you visualize her. First, she shouldn't look like your actual mother, or anyone else you know. She comes from a higher, spiritual world and isn't affiliated with any individual in your life.

But the most important thing in visualizing the Mother is this: she is the personification of love. Utterly serene, she radiates light and warmth. Some of my patients see her as a religious figure, like the Virgin Mother, or Aphrodite, the Greek goddess of love; others see her as an angel. Personally, because I'm not very good at visualizing, I don't actually "see" her; I feel her loving presence surrounding me and reaching directly into my heart.

Try the following exercise—repeating it several times if necessary—to find your own image or sensation of the Mother.

- Close your eyes and re-create the sense of demoralization you felt in the first exercise. Then turn it into a substance as you did in the second exercise.
- Imagine a loving Mother figure hovering a short distance above you. She exudes love, light, and warmth. What does she look like? How does it feel to be in her presence?
- Imprint this experience of the Mother in your memory so you can use it when you learn the tool.

Quite often, we find that just seeing the Mother gives a demoralized person a sense that they're not alone. But the Mother doesn't just want to keep you company; she wants you to realize your immense potential by removing the demoralization that stands in your way. She won't force you to give it to her—you must offer it up of your own free will. Once you do, she has the power to recycle it into something you need: unshakable faith in your potential. That's what the tool is for.

Now let's put it all together. Since you're going to use this tool when you feel crushed and hopeless, re-create those feelings right now. They are the starting point for the tool. Then walk yourself through the following steps slowly, taking time to feel each one.

THE MOTHER

TURN YOUR NEGATIVE THOUGHTS INTO A TOXIC SUBSTANCE: Feel the sense of demoralization as intensely as you can. Focus on its heaviness, as if it's an oppressive substance weighing you down. Visualize that substance so vividly that the demoralized thoughts and feelings are no longer in your head.

THE MOTHER APPEARS: See the Mother hovering above you. Place your faith in her power to remove the dark, heavy substance you're holding on to. Let go of it. The Mother lifts it from your body as if it's weightless. Watch it rise until it reaches her; she absorbs it into herself and it disappears.

FEEL HER LOVE: Now feel her eyes upon you. They radiate absolute confidence in you; she believes in you unreservedly, like no one else ever has. With her unshakable faith filling you up, everything feels possible.

How and When to Use the Mother

The Mother tool is remarkably easy to use. Here are a few tips to help you get the most out of it.

The first has to do with speed. Demoralization is like a boulder beginning to roll down a steep hill. The secret is to stop it the moment it starts to roll, so you prevent it from picking up speed. By the time it's halfway down the hill, it has so much momentum you will struggle to stop it. Get into the habit of using the Mother tool the moment negative thoughts and feelings start.

For example, let's say you get a bad review at work and your first thought is "I'm never going to amount to anything." What's your next step? Comb through all the evidence on which the review was based? Try to recall other times when your work was praised? Call a friend to complain about your boss? The answer: none of the above. The moment you have the negative thought, your job is to turn it into a substance and offer it up to the Mother. Remember, you are responsible for keeping yourself in a positive state, and you don't accomplish that by having an opinion about the thought or the event that triggered it; you accomplish it by using the tool immediately.

This requires a lot of discipline; inevitably there will be times when you forget to use the tool and slide into the hole. That doesn't mean you have to remain stuck. It just means you'll have to repeat the tool over and over again until the black mood passes. That takes faith, because when you're really down, you may not get immediate relief. But whatever happens, using the tool is superior to wallowing in hopelessness. Remember that you're in a fight with Part X, and if you don't fight back, you lose. I have treated patients who were so depressed they had to use the tool thirty times a day. Not one of them regrets it.

By the time she started therapy, Ann was ready to try anything. I guided her through the tool for the first time, and when she opened her eyes, she had tears welling, but this time they were tears of relief. "I don't know if I believe in any of this, but seeing the Mother's faith in me lifted me up." Ann kept using the tool multiple times each day. Initially, it provided only temporary relief. But she kept trying, and after a week, she noticed she was less despondent and more able to care for herself. A few weeks after that, she felt more like her old self. "I went out to lunch with a friend of mine who's really funny, and halfway through the meal I heard someone laughing. A second later I realized it was me."

DESTROYING FALSE HOPE BEFORE IT DESTROYS YOU

Ann had reached the point where she could consistently dispel her demoralization. She was back into her life, enjoying friends and activities, but she still had another hurdle to get over. It appeared as soon as a new man asked her out on a date. For a moment, her old hopelessness returned. "My first thought was 'Nooo way!' I never want to ride that roller coaster again."

Her reaction was understandable. Having your hopes raised and then dashed—over and over again—is devastating. Most people give up. They stop trying to make their dreams a reality. For Ann, that meant resigning herself to a life without romance. For others, it might mean giving up on a creative pursuit or a business venture. Usually, people justify it by saying they're just being "realistic," but the truth is, they're surrendering to Part X.

The answer is not to give up on your ambitions, but to pursue them in an entirely new way: your mood can't be contingent on their success or failure. Ann was halfway there. She'd learned to lift herself out of despair when a relationship ended. But she still needed to learn how to deflate her false hopes when a relationship began. False hopes are like phantoms, and in the words of author Virginia Woolf, "It is far harder to murder a phantom than a reality."

The first step was to learn to identify the false hopes. I urged her to start dating again, but with a completely different agenda. "Don't even think of it as a date. Think of it as an opportunity to study how Part X floods your mind with inflated expectations."

After her first date, she reported back to me. "I returned his call and the moment he answered I started to project into the future: 'He sounds great. . . . I wonder if he could be the one!' At dinner, I caught myself visualizing how he'd look in a wedding tux. By dessert I was positive he'd make a great father."

Ann was used to working on dark, depressing thoughts, but these overheated, excited ones were just as dangerous. They were Part X's way of luring her back into false hope. The next step was for Ann to do the same thing with these thoughts that she'd done with the demoralized ones: turn them into a substance. When I asked her to close her eyes and do this, she said the thoughts looked like the garish, dazzling lights of a

Vegas casino. I explained that they were as much of a barrier between her and the Mother as the black sludge of demoralization. Both impeded the Mother from helping Ann keep her balance. I instructed Ann to use the Mother tool whenever she felt overexcited about the prospect of a relationship.

But it's not so easy to destroy false hopes; it's like walking away from a bowl of your favorite candy. Ann went out on several more dates with the same guy, and when she came in again she was talking about him like he was a gift from God. "He's so good-looking, my friends all adore him, and you won't believe it—we're both into the same music!"

"Let me guess," I said. "You haven't been using the tool."

She looked startled for a second. "Oh, you mean the Mother tool. Well, come on. What's wrong with a few harmless fantasies? They make me feel good, especially after how depressed I've been!"

As a therapist, I find this kind of interaction very unsettling. It's as if the patient has forgotten everything they've learned—it's been wiped clean. In Ann's case, Part X had once again brainwashed her into believing that a guy was the answer. I don't enjoy shocking someone back into reality, but it feels even worse to collude with Part X when I know that eventually these false hopes will come crashing down. So I was tough on Ann.

"Are you fucking kidding me?" I said. She looked at me, wide-eyed. I went on: "Ann, it was the 'harmless fantasy' that Luke would keep your life exciting that landed you here in the first place. You were so demoralized you could barely get out of bed! Have you forgotten the lesson of that? If you use a fantasy to *elevate* your mood, at some point reality will send it crashing back down. Do you really want to go through that again?"

I leaned in and spoke more softly. "C'mon. You know this doesn't end well. Either this guy suddenly stops calling and you get depressed, or you get into a relationship and you get depressed at the six-month mark when it turns out you're still responsible for regulating your own mood."

She nodded; she couldn't disagree.

"I want you to use the Mother tool religiously, every single time you get overexcited about a relationship—with this guy or any other one—for the rest of your life."

Chastened, Ann followed my instructions. She went out on more dates, with different men, and found herself relating to each of them in an entirely new way. Instead of obsessively trying to figure out if he was "the one," for the first time she could sit back and enjoy getting to know someone.

Eventually, Ann found herself gravitating to one particular guy. Their relationship unfolded naturally and simply—two people drawing closer to each other without needing a guarantee about where it was going. After they'd been together for some months, Ann found herself getting a little bored, like she had with Luke. But this time, she used the Mother tool. She didn't get demoralized or even make that much of it. "It feels like the normal ups and downs of a relationship. I think we'll make it through this phase, but even if it ended, I'd still feel okay about my life."

THE GIFTS OF THE MOTHER

Like a human mother, the archetypal Mother gives birth. But she doesn't give birth to a child. She brings to life the priceless quality Ann found inside herself: an unshakable sense of optimism. No longer a leaf blowing this way or that depending on whether she was in or out of a relationship, Ann had found her roots in the Mother's unwavering love.

This is what makes the Mother tool so effective: when you see the Mother's absolute faith in you, you're filled with a radically new kind of hope. We call it "hopefulness."

Hopefulness isn't based on a future outcome. It's a positive attitude about the future—without knowing what it will bring. This may seem like a foreign concept, but you've already experienced it. Remember what it was like when you were a child and you'd wake up to a new day and couldn't wait to rush outside to play? You had no specific hopes or expectations; you were filled with the excitement of being alive.

Children have this kind of enthusiasm because Part X hasn't overtaken them yet. Without being aware of it, they're suffused with the love of the Mother. As we grow into adulthood, our task is to focus on the outside world, learning how to feed, clothe, and house ourselves, as well as relate to other people. Part X takes advantage of this outward orientation by convincing us there's a magical something that will ensure a bright future and make us happy forever. For Ann, that magical something was a relationship. For you, it might be having a child in the right school or selling a successful screenplay. Whatever it is, it will always fail to give you what you're looking for. That's what's "false" about false hope.

Hopefulness is true hope. It sustains you regardless of what might happen in the future. The Confessing Church—a German Protestant movement of the 1930s—used the following aphorism to inspire hope and perseverance in its opposition to the Nazis: "Even if I knew that the world was to end tomorrow, I would still plant an apple tree today." It is a statement that defies despair and chooses hopefulness, even when everything seems about to crash down around you.

But the Mother doesn't just help you with a healthy attitude about the future. She also helps you have a better attitude about people. The Mother, by constantly seeing the best in you, helps you see the best in others, even the most difficult people in your life. This kind of goodwill is the lifeblood of every relationship. When you see the potential in an inexperienced employee, you're more effective at helping her gain the skills she needs. When you're dealing with an inflexible bureaucrat and you can remember that he too is a child of the Mother, you're more likely to find a way past his obstinacy.

This is particularly important within families. Traditional psychology—with its fixation on the past—tends to blame our parents for all our difficulties. As you learned in Chapter 2, I was tempted to blame my mother for the pervasive feelings of failure I had. Once I established a true connection to the archetypal Mother and sensed her gazing at me confidently, I began to see my mother in a more balanced way. I could appreciate her strengths and forgive the areas in which she was weak.

After a while, your connection to the Mother changes

something even more profound: how you feel about yourself. You can never feel truly adult if whatever your parents did wrong continues to define you. You become a true emotional adult only when the archetypal Mother replaces your parents—and everyone else—as the source of your identity.

By far the greatest gift of the Mother is resilience. Resilience is one of the most important qualities a human being can possess. It's inevitable that life will knock you down— you might have to face divorce, job loss, or the death of someone you love. But if you stay down, your life will contract. That's where resilience comes in. It's the ability to pick yourself up quickly and keep expanding.

We all know people who face tremendous adversity and have a miraculous ability to keep going, but resilience isn't magic. It is the result of a specific creative ability: the power to create hope out of despair. Typically, when we think of creativity, we think of an activity that takes place in the outer world, like painting a picture, raising a child, or starting a business venture. Resilience requires a more primal creativity—it takes place in your inner world. It allows you to create hopefulness about the future no matter what you're facing in the present.

There's something paradoxical about this creative power. You don't learn it when things are going well; you learn it when the outside world disappoints you (the painting doesn't sell, the child develops a drug problem, the business goes belly-up). The weird truth is, you can't learn to pick yourself up unless you get knocked down. Our society doesn't help with this. It values only success, not failure. But every mother knows that failure is an essential part of growth, and that her child must fall down in order to learn how to walk. In the same way, the archetypal Mother knows that you must get demoralized so that you can possess the ultimate power: resilience.

CYCLES OF THE SOUL

Ann had learned a lot about resilience. Her breakup with Luke hadn't been the dead end she'd thought it would be. In fact, it led to an expansion of her life. She eventually married and started a family. They experienced the normal ups and downs of a married couple with kids, but Ann continued to use the Mother tool regularly to prevent Part X from taking over and flooding her with hopelessness.

Her career experienced a renaissance as well. An elementary school teacher, she'd always excelled at helping learning-disabled kids in her classroom. Now, with her renewed confidence, she'd applied for and received a promotion. She was now consulting for school districts all over the state. In every way, battling through demoralization with the Mother tool had increased her Life Force.

So you can imagine her surprise when, a few years later, she got depressed again. When she came to see me, she looked like she had in our first session: defeated. When I asked her what was wrong, she explained that her father had died suddenly of a heart attack. The death of a parent often crushes whatever false hopes we secretly hold on to—that he or she would finally take pride in our accomplishments, apologize for past wrongs, or say "I love you" for the first time. "I know it's crazy, but I guess I was still holding out hope that he'd be happy for what I've achieved, or at least that he'd ac-knowledge it. When he died, I realized that was never going to happen."

"Are you using the Mother tool?"

"I am, and it's helping. But there's something I don't get. I'm so much stronger than I was back then, when I first started seeing you. Why do I have to go through these hor-rible feelings all over again?"

The answer reveals one of the profound secrets of the Life Force. All of us wish that it could increase in a straight line, like our proficiency at a videogame. You achieve one level, advance to the next, and keep moving upward. Over time, you would never have to return to a previous level. According to this notion, Ann, having battled through her demoralization with Luke, would never have to sink into an-other episode of depression.

Here is a picture of this linear view of the Life Force:

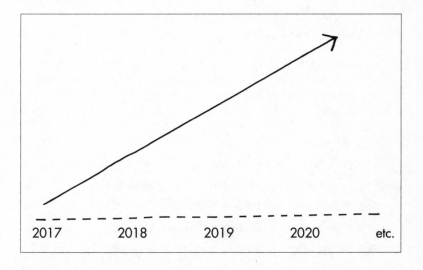

But that's not how life actually works. Remember: Part X, the enemy of life, is going to do everything it can to push you back down. It doesn't give up just because you've beaten it once. After Ann recovered from the breakup with Luke, Part X flooded her with inflated fantasies of what a new relationship could bring. After she destroyed those false hopes, Part X lay in wait until her father died, attacking her yet again. What this means is that although you can increase your Life Force, *you can increase it only in cycles.* To put it simply, life is two steps forward, one step back.

The cyclical view of the Life Force is depicted below:

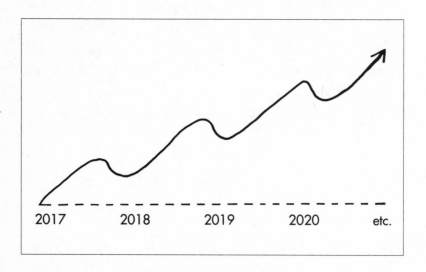

Overall, your Life Force is increasing, but there are still down periods when Part X pushes you back into a hole.

We want to state emphatically how important it is to accept the cyclical view of life. If you want to be fully alive—excited to get up in the morning, firing on all cylinders during the day, feeling like your life has purpose—you have to face the truth: there's always going to be a downturn, and you'll always have to fight your way back up again.

There's a priceless gift that comes with accepting that there's another hole waiting for you in the future: you're prepared for it. Moreover, you get better and better at climbing out of it each time. Demoralization derives much of its power from the sense that it lasts forever. If you ask people who are depressed, they'll admit they feel like they're never going to recover. But when you've lifted yourself out of despair over and over again, it loses its power over you. There's a bone-deep confidence that you can rise above anything. The existentialist philosopher Albert Camus put it beautifully: "In the depth of winter, I finally learned that within me there lay an invincible summer."

This discovery of an inner, invincible summer is more exciting than any external success you've ever achieved. External success always has an element of luck in it—there are many factors out of your control that have to come together for it to happen. But it's all *your* doing when you're able to turn things around inside you. The surge of Life Force that goes with this is incomparable. Phil and I have both had patients who've turned things around so many times they actually look forward to the next down phase; they're confident it's simply the prelude to living more fully than they ever have before.

The ancient Greeks had a much deeper appreciation for these cycles than we do. They depicted the cyclical nature of life in the myth of Persephone. Persephone was the daughter of Demeter, a Mother Earth goddess. One day, Hades, ruler of the underworld, abducted Persephone into his deathly realm. When Demeter discovered this, she was beside herself and demanded the return of her daughter, vowing that the earth would remain barren until then. Hades agreed, but tricked Persephone into eating pomegranate seeds before he released her. Because she had tasted the fruit of the underworld, Persephone was obligated to return there for several months every year. The Greeks believed that this explained the origin of winter, with its loss of fertility. It also accounted for the bursting renewal of spring upon her return.

What the ancient Greeks saw as happening in the realm of the gods now takes place within the soul of every human being. Each figure in the myth is a part of your psyche. The pomegranate seeds represent the false hopes that Part X (Hades) has planted inside us. Because of them, our Life Force (Persephone) cycles endlessly between two worlds. The underworld is the inner hell we create when we search for eternal happiness and end up deadened and demoralized. But the Mother (Demeter) is always there to bring us back to the world of light and life.

This is the human condition: Part X will inevitably succeed in abducting you into the realm of death and demoralization, but you also have the tools to fight your way back out again. Every time you do, you will find yourself living a more inspired life, one with a greater sense of purpose. In a sense, by falling down into the land of death, you admit that you need the Mother, who breathes even more life into you.

This also changes our notion of what it means to be heroic. We think of our heroes as people who *never* get demoralized. This just adds to our sense of shame and inferiority when we fall into the hole. The true hero is the one who *does* get demoralized, but who also develops the ability to bring himself or herself out of it.

In the twentieth century, one of the best examples of this kind of heroism was Martin Luther King, Jr. The last year of his life was marked with a deep sense of hopelessness, failure, and impending death. He was under attack from all sides. The FBI was wiretapping his phone calls, planting operatives in his organization, even sending anonymous letters urging him to kill himself. There were constant death threats, culminating in early 1968 when the FBI and local police warned him to curtail his public appearances.

But even more demoralizing to King was the fact that nonviolence seemed to be failing as a movement. Newark, New Jersey's most populous city, exploded with violence in July of 1967, and Detroit followed a week later. There were more than 125 riots by the end of that year. The black establishment thought King was going too far, and young black radicals derided him for not going far enough.

King had been plagued with depression all his life. Now he saw his mission—a free black people who stood on equal footing in a white society—failing. He began to ruminate on death, talking about it all the time. In August of 1967, he was so depressed he couldn't rouse himself to board a flight from Atlanta to Louisville. And yet, on April 3, 1968, the night before he was murdered, he delivered one of the most inspiring speeches of his career. He admitted that there would be difficult days ahead. "But," he declared, "it really doesn't matter with me now, because I've been to the mountaintop. . . . Like anybody, I would like to live a long life. Longevity has its place. But I'm not concerned about that now. I just want to do God's will. And He's allowed me to go up to the mountain. And I've looked over. And I've seen the promised land. I may not get there with you. But I want you to know tonight that we, as a people, will get to the promised land. And so I'm happy tonight. I'm not worried about anything. I'm not fearing any man."

King's ability to create hope out of despair and lift others with him marks him as one of the great leaders of the twentieth century. But in the twenty-first century, we'll need more than great leaders to give us hope. The Life Force isn't just for leaders—it's in each and every one of us—and it wants us to develop this ability ourselves. In a sense, relying on a great leader to rescue you from the abyss is just another version of false hope; it's relying on someone outside you, instead of the Life Force inside you. This is the whole reason tools are so important—it's why Phil and I are so fanatical about teaching our patients to use them. By doing so, they develop *their own* relationship with the Life Force, instead of remaining dependent on us for encouragement. They become complete, self-reliant individuals.

The heroes of the twenty-first century will be ordinary individuals—like you and me—who overcome their own sense of hopelessness and bring more to those who are caught in a web of difficulties. It might mean lifting the spirit of a family disheartened by a loss or setback; reconciling members of a community who've antagonized one another; nurturing the abilities of someone whose talents have gone unrecognized. Each act of kindness may seem unremarkable in itself, but put together they will enable the spirit of the

Mother to enter our society—connecting people to one another, lifting them out of despair, and, ultimately, increasing the amount of love in the world.

The mission of the modern individual is to bring the energies of the Mother—love, connectedness, compassion—into the world. In the final chapter of this book, we'll show you how your work lifting yourself out of the holes you fall into will help the entire world lift itself up.

FREQUENTLY ASKED QUESTIONS

I've been depressed for most of my life—it runs in my family. Is there a difference between the depression I suffer from and what you're calling demoralization?

Yes, there is. In this chapter, we're defining demoralization in terms of a very specific, three-step sequence that occurs in almost every individual. Step one is false hope: Part X gets you to believe there's a magical person or event that will relieve you of the responsibility to work on your own mood. For Ann, this was "the right guy," but it could be anything—getting pregnant, winning a promotion, graduating from a particular college, or achieving any other goal. Step two is the inevitable shattering of that hope: either you don't get what you want, or you do get it and discover it isn't magical—you still have to learn to sustain your own mood. Either way, you end up feeling demoralized, which is step three.

Depression is a much broader phenomenon than the specific three-step sequence we've described. In contrast to demoralization, depression can be caused by a wide-ranging combination of factors, including genetics, changes in hormone levels, certain medical conditions, stress, isolation, and other difficult life circumstances. Only some people are prone to depression, but almost everyone has felt demoralized when they suffered a setback—even if it was short-lived.

The Mother tool can help you regardless of whether you're suffering from demoralization or depression. However, ongoing, untreated depression can be very dangerous. If you have this condition and it persists, you should continue to use the tool, but you should also see a doctor for ongoing psychotherapy and/or medication.

When I get to step two of the tool, I find myself holding on to the dark substance; it's difficult to release it to the Mother. What should I do?

Part X has a variety of ways to prevent the tools from working. This is one of them. Its aim is always to keep you in the hole of demoralization and prevent you from climbing out. That's why it gets you to hold on to the dark substance instead of releasing it to the Mother.

The most important thing is to keep using the tool; don't give up. When you reach the point where you're called upon to give up the dark, heavy substance, slow down and give it to the Mother in little bits. Don't feel that you have to succeed at this on the first try. If you keep at it, eventually you'll be able to release all of the darkness.

It's valuable to examine what you feel as you give it up, bit by bit. Don't be surprised if you feel a sense of loss. That's to be expected. A dirty little secret of human nature is that most of us would rather molder in the dark hole of demoralization than make the effort to climb out of it. The reason for this is simple: if we're successful, and we recover from demoralization, there's no going back to our false hopes. Once the tool works, and you know you have the *ability* to regulate your own mood, you have to accept the truth: you're responsible for creating your own sense of optimism—you'll never find a magical something or someone that will relieve you of that responsibility. Like a toddler who's been clinging to his bottle, you're forced to graduate to solid food—and truth be told, you'll miss the bottle for a while.

It's understandable that this is difficult; you're venturing into new emotional territory. But don't give in. Even if it takes many tries to reach the point where you can give up all of the darkness and overcome the sense of loss, you'll be rewarded many times over. You'll reach true emotional adulthood.

If there's an archetypal Mother, is there also an archetypal Father?

Yes, there is. The next chapter will be devoted to understanding the archetypal Father. But for now, think of it as the force that shatters your false hopes. The Father does this not because he's punitive or cruel, but because he wants you to learn an invaluable skill—maintaining your inner state no matter what adversity he throws your way; he's training you to become a fully functioning adult, able to regulate yourself. To put it another way, the Father knocks you down so you'll rely even more heavily on the Mother, who gives you the power to pick yourself back up again. In the process, you become unstoppable.

OTHER USES OF THE MOTHER

THE MOTHER TOOL ALLOWS YOU TO UNBLOCK YOURSELF AND REACH A CREATIVE FLOW. To be fully alive, you must be creative. This is obvious if you're an artist, musician, or writer. But ordinary, everyday life requires innovation as well. It takes imagination to keep a romantic relationship alive, to resolve conflicts with your kids, to excel at your job, and so on. When you're connected to a creative flow, even the most mundane tasks are infused with a sense of newness and vitality. But there's a catch. You don't create anything by yourself—everything is co-created with the Mother; she is the source of the creative flow. The process by which that flow comes through you has many twists and turns—there are false starts, detours, and even dead ends that force you to start over. To remain in a creative flow, you cannot allow Part X to make these setbacks about you and your failings. If you make it about yourself, you will cut yourself off from the Mother. That's when you become creatively blocked. The twists and turns must be seen as a natural part of a process that you can't control. Your responsibility is simple: stay connected to the Mother no matter what happens.

Mark, an aspiring composer, got his first big break writing the theme music for a new TV show. Needless to say, he wanted to write a hit, so after reading the pilot he spent every day in his office trying to come up with the best music he'd ever written. At first, he had so many different ideas he could barely write them all down. But gradually, he began to find fault with each theme: one didn't fit the tone of the show; another took too long to resolve; a third felt derivative of another show he'd seen. As these obstacles began to pile up, Mark's initial enthusiasm was replaced with self-doubt and growing panic that he was going to blow his opportunity. This made things even worse: the ideas slowed to a trickle and soon he was spending more time catastrophizing than creating. By the time he came to see me, he was completely blocked. "I still show up and sit at my desk, but I'm paralyzed. I can't even remember what I used to love about music."

I explained that Part X is astonishingly good at shutting down a creative process. It does this by getting you to obsess about yourself. In this case, X flooded Mark with panic and self-loathing. But I've seen instances where a creative person wins an award or gets a positive review and gets equally obsessed—he can't resume creating until he takes the focus off himself. As a creative person, the only thing you're allowed to be obsessed with is maintaining your connection with the Mother. Staying connected to her ensures that you'll be able to maximize your creative potential.

This meant that Mark had to use the Mother tool consistently. Every time he started to criticize himself or panic about his future, he turned the thoughts and feelings into a dark substance and gave them up to the Mother. In a remarkably short time, he began to get ideas again.

But that didn't mean he was done using the tool. I explained to him that all ideas, in their raw form, are imperfect, and that Part X would want to use whatever was "wrong" to return to self-obsession. I told him he had to change his expectations of the creative process—he had to *expect* the ideas to be imperfect, use the Mother tool, and bring even more creativity to the imperfect ideas. "Nothing you ever create will be perfect. But the imperfection isn't an excuse to obsess about yourself, it's a trigger to connect even more deeply to the Mother."

THE MOTHER TOOL ALLOWS YOU TO FEEL GOOD ABOUT YOURSELF, REGARDLESS OF OTHERS' OPINIONS OR HOW THEY TREAT YOU. Just about everyone has somebody in their life who's impossible to please. It could be your parent, teacher, boss, or anyone else. Part X convinces you that you must win over this person— it's the only way to make yourself feel worthy. This form of false hope is disastrous because you lose either way. If you don't get the person's approval, you feel terrible, and if you do get a tidbit every now and then, you'll crave even more. You're caught, like a hamster on an exercise wheel, running as fast as you can and getting nowhere.

When Grace was hired at her law firm, she was as highly qualified as any candidate they'd ever considered. There was almost no honor she hadn't achieved: editor of the law review at an Ivy League school, Order of the Coif, a clerkship with one of the toughest Supreme Court justices, etc. On day one, she was assigned to one of the senior partners of the firm. At first, Grace was thrilled—her new boss, the scion of a long line of esteemed lawyers, was one of the hardest-hitting litigators in the country; she would be learning from the best. Whenever she mentioned she was going to be working for him, however, other attorneys would roll their eyes and wish her luck. Anyone else might have been daunted, but Grace was always up for a challenge; her enthusiasm was undimmed.

Six months later, she came to see me. She looked haggard, like she hadn't slept in months. Worse, she was feeling something she'd never felt before: terrible about herself. "Nothing I do pleases him. Come to think of it, the only time I've ever seen him smile was when he was ripping into an assistant about a mistake she'd made; he actually seemed to be enjoying himself."

As we explored her relationship with her boss, one thing became clear: the more he withheld his approval, the harder she tried to gain it, staying at work later than everyone else, finding obscure precedents, coming up with novel litigation strategies, and so on. Nothing worked. "When I succeed at something, he acts like it's nothing special. In fact, he almost seems disappointed, like he secretly wanted me to fail so he could berate me!" It was like a sadomasochistic relationship without the sex.

I told her that her boss was a vicious animal whose sole pleasure was torturing everyone under him. "You'll never make him happy, you'll never get his approval, and it's self-destructive to keep trying. He's like a cannibal—but instead of eating your flesh, he'll consume your self-esteem. He's already about halfway there." I explained that he'd been sent into her life to introduce her to the Mother—the only true source of love and approval—and I explained how to use the Mother tool. I instructed her to use it whenever she wanted his approval. "Expect nothing but contempt from him—get everything you need from the Mother."

Not surprisingly, Grace was very disciplined about using the tool. The hard part was feeling the Mother's love. She was used to *earning* approbation: she won her teachers' praise by going above and beyond assignments, her parents' approval by being well behaved, her friends' loyalty by offering a shoulder to cry on. The Mother's love was *unearned*. "I feel like I don't deserve it." It took time for Grace to get used to the notion that the Mother loves everyone and everything without judgment; her love is like the air we breathe—it's available regardless of merit. As Grace began to let her love in, she began to feel better about herself—in an unprecedented way. She stopped defining herself in terms of how other people treated her. We knew she'd succeeded when her boss, sensing that Grace no longer cared what he said or did, reassigned her to work for another senior partner.

THE MOTHER TOOL HELPS YOU RECOVER FROM THE DARK MOODS THAT OFTEN ACCOMPANY PHYSICAL ILLNESS OR FATIGUE.
Your body is a natural bulwark against Part X; its fitness and vitality give you a foundational energy with which to maintain an optimistic attitude. But when something goes wrong with your body, it's easy to lose your footing. Anything that

> compromises your strength—the flu, an infection, an injury—can put you in a hole, even if you're not prone to demoralization. Chronic conditions—arthritis, cancer, Crohn's disease, asthma, etc.—are even worse; Part X uses the condition's permanence to flood you with dark feelings. The Mother bypasses your body—reaching directly into your soul—and lifts you out of the sense of hopelessness. She infuses you with the ability to move forward; despite your body's limitations, you can feel the pure joy of being alive.

Jenna had been healthy for most of her life. A competitive swimmer in her youth, she'd always kept herself in top-notch physical condition. But now, in her late fifties, she had begun to experience chronic back pain. Her doctor had ruled out all the obvious causes, and Jenna had tackled the problem with the can-do attitude she brought to every other obstacle in her life: consistent exercise and stretching, acupuncture and massage treatments, anti-inflammatories, alternating cold and hot packs, etc. Although these provided temporary relief, it was beginning to sink in that the pain might never go away. "I've never had to face anything like this before. The pain is always there—I can't get my mind off it. Then I start thinking, 'It's only going to get worse,' and I slide into this hole I can't bring myself out of."

I told Jenna the truth: each of us reaches a point in life where we can't rely on a brighter future to bring us hope, because there's no guarantee that the future will be better. In fact, given that the deterioration of our bodies is inevitable, you can be certain that from a physical point of view, the future is going to get worse. It's at this point in life that you must rely on something stronger than predictions of a good future: you must rely on the Mother's ability to raise you up in the present. I taught Jenna the tool and asked her to turn not only her pessimistic thoughts but the physical pain itself into a substance that was getting in between her and the Mother. As the Mother absorbed her pain and worry, she felt lighter and more optimistic; even the physical pain was easier to bear.

SUMMARY

HOW PART X ATTACKS YOU: *It floods you with feelings of hopelessness that are so strong you give up pursuing your dreams. Certain you'll never get what you want, you stop trying.*

HOW THIS DEADENS YOU: *When you give in to despair, you destroy your ability to create the kind of future you want. Your answer to everything becomes "Why bother?"*

HOW PART X TRICKS YOU INTO GIVING IN: *On an unconscious level, Part X convinces you that there is a magical something—a good relationship, wealth, a particular job—that, once attained, will exempt you from your responsibility to maintain an open, optimistic view of the future. Once this "false hope" is crushed, X floods you* *with despair, and convinces you there's no antidote. You are "alive," but only in the biological sense.*

THE SOLUTION: *The Mother tool creates hope out of despair. It gives you the resilience to bounce back from any defeat, no matter how great. Your relationship with the Mother becomes an unwavering source of support and confidence in your future.*

Chapter Six

The Tool: The Tower

Have you ever felt hurt or wronged by someone and felt like retaliating or retreating into a victim state? Phil shows you how you can instead reopen your heart and move forward.

Before I even saw Andrew, I heard his voice. It preceded him into my office as if it were announcing the presence of an important person. When he walked through my door—with his silver hair, strong features, and resonant baritone—he could have easily been taken for a captain of industry or a political figure. In reality, he was a TV anchorman for a local station.

He introduced himself with the practiced quality of someone in the public eye, flashing a thousand-watt smile that conveyed how thrilled he was to be there. He talked nonstop, and the topic of conversation was me. He knew a great deal about me—too much as far as I was concerned. My education, books and articles I'd written, where to find me online. The whole thing was a transparent effort to get my approval, done with such enthusiasm it was impossible not to like him.

But when I ignored his words and looked in his eyes, I saw shock and confusion. It was the look you'd expect from a soldier in the middle of a surprise attack.

When I asked him why he'd come to see me, the perfect smile turned to a grimace and his voice became that of a frightened sixteen-year-old.

"At my job . . . they're trying to kill me." He saw me scrutinizing him. "No, no . . . not literally kill me. In TV that's what they say when they try to ruin you."

As if to illustrate his point, he held his heart, the way you do when you say the Pledge of Allegiance, only he held it with both hands like he was trying to hold in blood oozing from a chest wound. There was no blood, just pain.

"What happened?" I asked him.

"Ratings were down last year, so they hired a new co-anchor, Kelly. She's . . ." He choked on his own words.

It wasn't hard to know where this was going, so I filled in the spaces for him: "Young, attractive, and ambitious?"

"And really smart. I know it sounds like a cliché."

"She's the one who's wants you dead?"

"I'm not sure. . . . It's complicated." He went on to describe a host of unnecessary details about Kelly without getting to the point of the story. I told him to stop entertaining me and just tell me what happened.

We were thirty minutes into the first session, and most psychiatrists would have already diagnosed Andrew as a narcissist (or, technically, as having a narcissistic personality disorder). But just as there are many breeds of dogs, narcissists come in many flavors. Andrew loved the attention he got from performing for others; it didn't matter where. Every bar, restaurant, park bench, etc., has seen someone like Andrew holding court.

There's a darker kind of narcissist who pursues power and success at all costs. They're more than willing to take advantage of other people and don't seem to care about—or even be aware of—the effect they have on others. It's as if they're missing a part of their soul. That was not Andrew. Underneath his façade, he was fragile and unsure; he used attention to hide his insecurity from others. Of course, drawing attention to yourself isn't the best way to hide your failings, especially when your face is seen by throngs of viewers every day—but it was all he knew.

Kelly being hired was a problem for Andrew before she even arrived. He'd been at the station for some years and expected a say in who'd be on camera with him, but he hadn't been consulted. "I'm the one who has to work with her, but no one ever asked my opinion. It's not fair."

Fairness had nothing to do with it. His bosses didn't want Andrew at the strategy meetings because he'd hog the floor, telling war stories that had nothing to do with the matter at hand. Andrew had no idea how others were reacting to him. His misinterpretation of not being invited to the meetings was "I go out of my way to be helpful and they ignore me." But that wasn't something he'd dare say to his bosses; he needed their approval too much.

Andrew's need for validation wasn't new; he'd spent his childhood trying and failing to win his father's approval. His father was a hard-bitten newspaper reporter who didn't care

how many toes he stepped on to get a story. A talented journalist, he never got his own column because he'd made too
many enemies.

His father was highly critical of Andrew, berating him for
not going all out for anything in life. "You're so afraid of getting hurt all you do is feel sorry for yourself." His father
could just as well have been talking about himself. A bitter
man, he warned Andrew never to trust anyone, telling him,
"Watch your back." That philosophy didn't make Andrew
tougher; it made him afraid of people.

Andrew was physically imposing, but his soul was timid
and hypersensitive. If a teacher criticized him, a girl wouldn't
dance with him, or—worst of all—someone didn't laugh at
his jokes, he'd replay the rejection in his imagination until it
was all he could think about.

A journalism major, but soured by his father's experience
with print, Andrew went into broadcasting. His looks agreed
with the camera enough for him to find an anchor job at a
local station. His father was unimpressed; he considered TV
news the domain of empty-headed pretty boys.

At that point, Andrew gave up on getting support or encouragement from his father. Since he was only able to feel
good about himself in the act of entertaining others and
basking in their appreciation, his best audience became the
crew at the station, who took it as a compliment that he'd
even hang out with them. Andrew's ultimate goal was to
have his own show. To accomplish that, he'd have to impress
his bosses, and they were a much tougher audience than the
crew.

Andrew's need to be liked made him a "soft" interviewer.

Rather than work a guest over with hard questions, he'd let them off the hook. This was a disappointment to the viewers who wanted blood, or at least some juicy revelations, and a disappointment to his bosses, who wanted better ratings.

One of the producers, an older man, saw Andrew's potential and took him under his wing. His new mentor didn't sugarcoat things, telling him he needed more gravitas to be taken seriously. "Do you want to be the king or the court jester?" was how he put it. Andrew wouldn't gain authority reading from a teleprompter—he had to go into the field and produce something original, something with his name on it. The exposure terrified him.

He convinced himself to do it, but the interview hadn't gone deep enough and the piece wasn't well received. His mentor wanted him to try again, but Andrew refused, saying he preferred to stick to what he knew he could do: reading the news from a teleprompter.

His mentor said he couldn't help unless Andrew was willing to take risks. Rather than admit he was terrified, Andrew complained, "No one believes in me."

It was about this time that Kelly was hired. Andrew—wanting Kelly to like him—told her everything he knew about the job. She was effusively grateful, but in the back of his mind was his father's admonition to trust no one.

Not needing to be loved, Kelly was willing to make on-air guests uncomfortable. The audience liked the sharp edge she gave the show—the sense she was on the verge of catching someone with something to hide. The ratings went up almost immediately. Within her first six months, they gave Kelly her own show. Andrew couldn't understand how it was awarded to someone with so much less experience. *It wasn't fair.*

Andrew, in his best the-world-is-against-me mode, was certain Kelly had manipulated her way into the job. He confronted his ex-mentor and demanded to know why he hadn't protected him from getting stabbed in the back by Kelly.

"She never did a thing to hurt you. All she did was to prepare well and take risks. She was willing to be uncomfortable; you just want to be liked."

Retelling this story in my office affected Andrew in a way nothing else could: he became silent.

"What are you going to do?" I asked him.

"Damned if I know."

"That's progress."

I wasn't kidding. When you're wrong enough times, you're forced to admit you need to look at life in a new way. The first step was for him to stop blaming the world for his troubles.

THE PROBLEM: BEING A VICTIM

We call what Andrew went through an "injury." Physical injury, which is how most people who aren't shrinks use the term, is when you break a bone or you cut your finger chopping vegetables. But there are psychological injuries too: a friend questions your loyalty; you get a rejection letter from graduate school; you get thoroughly ignored at a social event. These injuries are every bit as painful as physical injuries.

Psychological injuries involve emotional rather than physical pain. Because we can't "see" the inner wound causing the pain, we downplay the effect psychological pain has on us. "Sticks and stones will break my bones, but words can never hurt me," is folk wisdom that seems so obvious we don't think to challenge it. But we should. In real life, words of rejection, contempt, and disrespect can hurt us just as surely as a fall down a long flight of stairs.

In one sense, psychological pain is *worse* than physical pain. The forces that heal a broken bone operate outside your awareness or control—it heals itself. Unless there are complicating factors, the pain goes away as you heal.

Psychological injuries don't heal so automatically. The reason: Part X doesn't want them to heal—quite the opposite, in fact. Rather than heal injuries you already have, it wants you to experience new ones. Its goal is to submerge you in so much pain your soul shrinks and your potential is destroyed.

For Part X, every experience of hurt feelings is an opportunity to cripple you further. We all know people—some very close to us—who get their feelings hurt constantly. If you look beyond any one complaint, a pattern emerges: these people are actually *collecting injuries*. The sense of being hurt by lovers, friends, family, and others defines them. When they tell others in detail about how they've been hurt, they're like an art a collector showing off their collection.

Andrew had his own version of this. He loved to entertain people with jokes and stories about celebrities, but the conversation would always end up with him complaining about the latest mistreatment in his life, whether it was by his unsupportive father or his unappreciative bosses. He was so entertaining and upbeat, even when complaining, that it was hard to tell he was hiding his real identity—that of a victim.

Victims feel put upon by the world. They're in a passive state: they think things are done to them, not by them. There's an art to being a victim, a perverse creative process in which you make up excuses for your inability to move forward in life. Like Andrew, the victim has a battle cry of "It's not fair!"

But how does victimhood suck you in with such power and refuse to let you go? It's the product of a brilliant trap set by Part X. It sets its trap by playing on a universal weakness in human nature: our expectations about how the world should treat us.

Here are some common examples:

- You expect your daughter to respect your personal possessions and you feel violated when she "borrows" your makeup without asking.
- You expect your friends to keep their commitments and feel deserted when a friend who promised to help you move bails out at the last minute.
- You've been instrumental in helping a coworker advance his career; when you find yourself up for a promotion, you expect his help. Instead he pursues the position for himself.
- You've been in love with your partner for several years and expect it to proceed to marriage, but suddenly they announce they're interested in someone else.

Each of these people has a picture of the treatment they expect from others—loyalty, commitment, respect, etc. Their expectations seem reasonable to them, but that doesn't mean the other person would agree. Even if they did, they might not act in accordance with those expectations. Yet we persist in the fantasy that those around us will treat us the way we think is "right."

Why should the world treat you the way you think it should? You might as well say it should rain tomorrow because it's one of your expectations. The idea that something will happen because you expect it to happen is one of Part X's most destructive cons—the suggestion that you are special.

What does it mean to be special? The universe consists of an endless number of beings, each of which has its own place and its own mission. Peace of mind and a sense of meaning come from accepting your individual role in this vast scheme. The person who believes they are special refuses to submit to this order. They envision themselves to be at the very center of the universe, with everything revolving around them. From this made-up position, they have the magical power to determine how the rest of the universe treats them, as if they were God handing down the Ten Commandments.

You may have no conscious awareness of this assumption, but it dictates how you act and feel. It's disappointing to discover that specialness is a grand illusion. The world no more revolves around you than the sun revolves around the earth. What you're really seeing is Part X setting its trap.

X knows the rest of the world won't play by your rules, and each time it doesn't, you lose a little of your specialness.

But X offers you a way to make up for your loss—a new way to be special that doesn't depend on the loyalty, commitment, or respect of others. This other specialness isn't the result of being immune to injuries, it's the result of *being unable to avoid them.* If the world goes through the trouble of injuring you so often, you must be very important. Every experience of disrespect or rejection becomes proof that the universe has singled you out for special punishment. If you didn't have some sort of cosmic significance, why would it bother?

You're no longer singled out as a god; you're singled out as a victim. But you're still being singled out. Human beings can accept either reason to single themselves out; what they can't accept is *not to be singled out at all.* It leaves them feeling that they don't exist. That's why victims are so driven to collect injuries—it's their only way to remain special.

When you think of someone in your life who "takes things too personally," it means they see every event as a referendum on their specialness. If you hear someone saying things like "I can't catch a break," or "I would never treat them the way they treated me," you know they are caught in Part X's "victim trap."

THE BLACK MAGIC OF REINJURY

Victimhood isn't just a conclusion or a complaint; it's a deep inner feeling, as difficult to get rid of as a tattoo. Why doesn't it just wear itself out? After all, how many injuries can one suffer? Part X doesn't need a huge number of injuries to make you feel like a victim. In a kind of black magic, it can take a single injury and keep its victimizing effect going. In its final and most diabolical part of the trap, *you make yourself into a victim.*

You do this by repeating—to yourself—the details of an injurious event. In the same way that watching a horror film over and over keeps the horror alive inside you, when you "rewatch" the injury in your own imagination, it keeps the pain of the experience alive.

We call this process of telling the story over and over "reinjury." The intense retelling of an injury brings back the pain you felt at the time. The injury may have been in the past, but the pain of reliving it is in the present. There's no time limit on these reinjuries. Patients have come to see me because they can't stop reliving events from months, some-times years, before, and the pain remains just as bad. They've been wallowing in their pain while life passes them by.

If you stub your toe on a rock, creating physical pain, you wouldn't kick it again. Yet that's exactly what you do when you replay a psychological injury. Replaying what happened keeps you in pain as much as kicking the rock would. Why would you want to torture yourself this way? Because Part X has convinced you that to remain special you need to feel you're being injured every moment. Part X keeps the focus on you by picking a terrible event from your life, setting up the projector, and running it 24/7 in order to keep you in a state of constant pain.

Humans are plagued by the habit of holding on to wounds. In most of the world, tribal and ethnic divisions are main-tained by memories (accurate or not) of ancient wounds that must be avenged. The wounds have a sacred quality; they give meaning and purpose to a group or nation. There is no attempt to process these injuries and get past them. Quite the opposite: they are honored and re-experienced over and over. At their worst, they are used to justify terrorism, war, and mass murder.

One of Freud's early psychoanalytic "cures" involved reliving the patient's original trauma by retelling it to the therapist. The idea was that if you relived it enough times, the problems that stemmed from them would disappear. Let's say your father left your family and remarried, abandoning you and your mother. Your therapist would have you tell this story over and over again with the presumption that in the retelling you would find healing.

What the theory failed to recognize was that Part X uses the same process for its own ends. Each time you retold this story of early abandonment, you were reinjuring yourself. It made no difference that it was taking place in a therapist's office. It would be like trying to cure a broken arm by going to a doctor's office and breaking it all over again.

Nonetheless, the technique of reliving the past has been widely accepted as a psychotherapeutic technique. Its acceptance isn't based on its effectiveness. The warm reception it has enjoyed is because it advances Part X's agenda. In a sense, Freud had an invisible colleague that hijacked the whole process: Part X. It co-opted a process meant to free people from past wounds and used it to create more victims.

THE PRICE OF VICTIMHOOD

Victims live limited lives. Their abilities to relate to others, to seize opportunities and take risks, and to live in a committed and meaningful way are all compromised. Their picture of themselves and others is blurred, leaving them disconnected and isolated.

Relationships

One of the few things more painful than being a victim is being around one. Listening to their nonstop complaints can be torture. Victims—and the hidden sense of specialness that drives them—are inner-oriented, but not in a good way. Solid, lasting relationships require you to go beyond your personal needs and become sensitive to what others are feeling, particularly how *you* make them feel.

But if your focus is purely on yourself, that's impossible. If you're the special one at the center of the universe, it's not important what anyone else is feeling; they don't matter. So although victims affect everyone around them, they have little or no awareness of what that effect is.

It's actually easy to identify someone who's in a victim state: they're unpleasant to be around. What's more difficult is to be aware of how others feel when *you* are in the victim state. As a victim, you are unable to process pain and move beyond it. Instead, you inflict your pain on those around you. Through "Woe is me" stories about mistreatment, complaints about the nature of the world, personal grievances, etc.—we call these "pain injections"—you force others to absorb the pain you should be processing yourself. Beyond putting others through undeserved agony, when you do this you are weakening the foundation of the entire relationship.

Let's say you're having a problem with your boss. You go to a close friend and download a feverish litany of his abusive acts: he yells at you, he demands that you go on personal errands for him, and so on. If she's a real friend, she'll immediately assume you need help. She'll worry about you, try to reassure you, maybe suggest a course of action. But if you're a victim, you don't want help; you just want to display your collection of injuries.

You dismiss whatever course of action your friend advises, because you didn't want to solve the problem, you just wanted a place to dump your garbage and validate your victimhood. Help is actually dangerous for victims—if they let it in, life might get better and they'd lose their special identity as a victim.

One of the primary goals of Part X is to destroy human relationships. If it can break the ties of love and loyalty that bind us together, it is free to attack person by person. Alone, no individual can win the battle with X. With its usual demonic genius, it has driven you to give your friend a double message: *I need help but I won't accept it.*

The more the friend loves you, and the more willing they are to take action to help you, the more confused and hurt this message makes them. Unintentionally, you have demeaned their love and goodwill. The friend leaves each interaction feeling worse than when it started. This is why victims end up complaining that their friends won't listen to them anymore.

Early in my career, I had an experience that taught me

the destructive power this Part X double message could unleash. I was treating an unpublished novelist with a high
opinion of himself and no income. He was running out of
savings, but getting a day job was beneath him. He'd walk
into each session complaining bitterly about the publishing
industry, the high cost of living, my not understanding him,
and so on. I worked my hardest to suggest options, even if
temporary, that could keep him alive financially until something sold.

But in the tradition of a victim, he radiated the "I need
help but I won't accept it" double message. Being inexperienced, I took his cry for help seriously and kept throwing out
suggestions. He shot down each one with a condescending
smirk that said, "How could you be so stupid?" Finally I
snapped. Jumping out of my chair, I heard a voice screaming,
"I've had enough!"

It was my voice. My reaction was so unexpected and ex-
plosive we both were stunned. A moment later, he got up and
made a quick exit, probably asking himself what kind of mad-
man he'd selected as a therapist. I learned from this how
powerfully Part X spoke through the state of victimhood.
Unchecked, it destroys relationships altogether, leaving the
victim isolated and hopeless.

Opportunity

One of most common complaints victims make is of lack
of opportunity. They'll often point out people they know who
are more successful than they are, not because of luck or talent or hard work, but because the person has "connections."
There's some truth in this, but what's more true is that con-

nections might get you a foot in the door, but you will very quickly be judged solely by the value you bring to the situation.

Whether it's not having the right partner or house or job, a victim always perceives a lack of opportunity. What they forget is that *they* are the cause of this lack. Opportunities don't come out of thin air; they come from interacting with other people. Meeting a potential spouse, finding an investment opportunity or a business partner, finding a mentor or a great teacher—all these things come via interactions with others.

This is a form of "street knowledge," not because someone sitting on a stoop disseminates it, but because the street is a metaphor for any public space where people can meet, including virtual spaces. It's as if there's a living generator of opportunities made of human beings interacting with one another. When a victim alienates people, they cut themselves off from this source. They really do have fewer opportunities, but only because they've created a self-fulfilling prophecy that confirms their skewed vision of the world. Andrew, who had slowly distanced himself from his bosses and was unwilling to try again after failure, found himself, by his own accord, with fewer opportunities and the sense that his bosses, his co-anchor, and even his mentor were out to get him.

Timidity

Damaged by the pain they've suffered in the past, most victims are terrified of suffering more pain in the future. They stay in a job, a marriage, or a friendship, but they just go through the motions, not giving it their all. They rationalize this by convincing themselves they don't care or even by recasting ambition as something crass or vulgar. Andrew chose another rationalization: why keep trying when you know it's going to fail?

Caring carries with it the potential for hurt feelings. If you write a blog, you may get nasty comments on it. If you choose an unusual career, your friends and family might look down on you. If you have a serious talk with your teenager, they may roll their eyes like you're an idiot. To protect themselves, victims stop taking these risks, eventually abandoning their most cherished dreams in an attempt to avoid pain. What they get in exchange is a life of timidity—one that is "safe" and limited.

Timidity carries a huge price tag. You have a limited amount of time here on earth. Every moment that you aren't "all in" and fully committed is a wasted moment. The longer you live a "safe" life, the more your goals, potential, and any sense that your life has meaning all fade away and eventually seem beyond reach. You've consigned your soul to Part X.

The only way to take it back is to identify what's really important to you and pursue it with every last ounce of energy. There's a risk in this: when you pursue life with this level of commitment and you get injured, it really hurts. That doesn't mean it's not worth it.

A great life is not one without injuries. A great life is one in which you risk great injuries and overcome them when they happen, again and again. The more willing you are to risk getting hurt, the more you'll have the expansive, opportunity-filled life you want. If you remain small because you're terrified of hurt, failure, or rejection—as Andrew did—you'll live a limited, disengaged, fearful life.

THE LIE THAT KEEPS US VICTIMS

This fear of emotional injury is universal. But what makes that fear so intense? It's Part X lying to us about the nature of pain. The lie is that *pain can kill you.* It can't—but to the degree it feels like it can, you become its prisoner. You probably haven't seen anyone die of pain recently, so where does this idea come from? It's the product of Part X stirring up the most primal human fear and inserting it where it doesn't belong. This fear—of course—is of death.

What is death? For most of us it's a mysterious, incomprehensible void, so much bigger and deeper than we're accustomed to that we can't describe it or claim to know its meaning. It's like trying to describe what you see while standing at the edge of a cliff looking out into pitch darkness. In one sense, there's nothing to describe; in another sense, the whole universe stands in front of you. You can feel it, but you can't understand it.

But we modern human beings have a hard time admitting there are things we don't understand. So we think of death in a way that fits in with what we experience in our own life. And in our experience, people we know die. They're not "here" anymore; they don't come back. It doesn't matter where they might be, or if they're nowhere at all. What matters is that whatever they were doing—even if it was just surviving—is over, finished. Life holds no more at-bats for them: no more opportunities to apologize, no more tries to lose weight, no more chances to read that novel. *Death is a final state.*

But there's another kind of death: the death of your ego. The ego is the source of your individual identity, the way you want the world to see you. When your feelings get hurt, when you get "dissed" or criticized, the injury is to your ego. When Andrew said, "They're killing me," the death was emotional, not physical. But he said it with the crushed sense of finality we associate with death. This was the end and there was nothing he could do about it—the exact thing that makes death so frightening.

Although hurt to the ego *feels* like a physical death, it's not. Part X has connected two things that have nothing to do with each other. It has taken the finality of physical death and applied it to your hurt feelings. The result: when you experience an injury, you feel like you're going to die.

Logically, you should be less afraid of ego injury than of physical injury. But Part X—with its usual destructive brilliance—blurs the distinction between the two and maintains the illusion that emotional pain can kill you.

How can you uncross the wires? *You get rid of the illusion that pain will kill you by letting it kill you.* You need to let the pain in and feel it fully. What will die is your ego and it's your ego that's keeping you from your own Life Force—the force that will allow you to recover from injury.

You can't experience pain by thinking about it. To feel pain you need your heart, not your head. The heart accepts pain without judgment, including pain in every form imaginable: hurt, rage, humiliation, sadness, frustration, etc. Because it connects to the Life Force, the heart has the ability to recover from even the deepest hurts.

Children are our best examples of the life-giving power of an open heart. If a child has their heart set on a toy and the parent refuses to buy it, they might burst into uncontrollable sobbing. But in a very short time, that same child will move on to the next activity, and soon after that they're smiling and happy. They desired the toy passionately, and they cried passionately. Their open-heartedness allows them to feel the pain, move through it, and recover.

As we grow older we stop experiencing the world through our hearts and start knowing it with our heads. The head can make judgments about a painful event, but it can't truly experience it. Fortunately, our hearts are not fully lost to us.

To reach them, we need the help of a tool that reawakens the heart's ability to accept and transform pain. We call it the Tower. It teaches you to see an injury not as a death, but as a portal into a more expansive life. Once you master it, you'll stop dealing with pain as a victim. You'll have the strength and courage to move through injuries and come out the other side. Pain will no longer be an obstacle but an opportunity.

THE TOOL: THE TOWER

To learn the tool, you'll need to pick a situation where your feelings were hurt, an instance where you were wounded badly enough that the pain stayed around for a while. It doesn't matter how old you were or who hurt you. Once you've re-created the incident and can feel your hurt feelings intensely, you're ready to use the tool.

THE TOWER

DEATH: Call up the hurt feelings that you just identified. Make them much worse and feel them attacking you right in your heart. They become so intense that your heart breaks and you die. You are left lying motionless on the ground.

ILLUMINATION: You hear a voice that says with great authority, "Only the dead survive." The moment it speaks, your heart fills with light, illuminating your surroundings. You see you are lying at the bottom of a hollow tower, which is open at the top. The light from your heart spreads through the rest of your body.

TRANSCENDENCE: Buoyed by the light, you effortlessly float up the tower and out the top, continuing your ascent into a perfect blue sky. Your body, purified of all pain, feels completely new.

The Tower makes it possible for you to succeed at the ultimate creative act—the creation of a new version of yourself. The tool harnesses the ability of the heart to transform even the darkest feelings. In the ancient world, this transformative power of the heart was hidden from the average person—it was the province of the gods and the spiritual elite. In the modern world, it is open to each of us.

Every time you use the tool, you're changing the meaning of pain. Before, you associated pain with the finality of death. Now, pain becomes the portal into a limitless life. Instead of pain being something you're afraid of, it becomes something you can embrace. This is the essence of courage— not to avoid pain, but to feel it as a prelude to rebirth. The tool does more than talk about rebirth, it gives you a way to feel it.

The Tower allows you to feel the spiritual reality that there's always something after death. To make sure you can feel that, use the tool three times, one right after the other, each time faster than the time before. By the third time you use the tool, there is almost no gap between death and rebirth.

The first time, do it just as we've described. The second time, condense the tool to two steps. The first step combines experiencing the hurt feelings entering your heart with seeing yourself lying dead on the ground. The second step combines hearing the "Only the dead survive" voice with ascending up the tower.

The third time, do the two combined states as quickly as you can, too fast to visualize any details. It should have the cadence of one-two: pain-ascent or death-life. The secret of the tool is that it's okay to be afraid, *as long as fear isn't the last thing you feel.* No matter how deep or painful the wound is, the tool always ends with an effortless ascent up the tower.

For most people, using the tool represents a completely new way to deal with pain. It links death and rebirth: the worse the pain, the more inspiring it is to let it kill you and allow yourself to be reborn. The reason we speed up the cadence is so you can *feel* the link between the two phases. You're creating a habit that says we *always* feel rebirth after death; we always feel transcendence after pain.

How and When to Use the Tower

There are many more uses for the Tower than you might think. We encounter big and small injuries every day, and the sooner you use the tool, the quicker you can get out of the trap of the victim state.

The most obvious time to use the tool is the moment someone hurts your feelings, even if it's a small injury—if, for example, your best friend forgets your birthday, your boss doesn't like a report you wrote, or someone posts an embarrassing picture of you online. Part X doesn't care about the size of the hurt; it will use anything, no matter how small, to make you into a victim. What matters is how fast you use the tool. The speed with which you respond sends a message to Part X that you won't be conned by its lies anymore.

For most of us, using a tool is an unusual way to deal with our wounds. Because of that, when we start out, very often we will miss the first cue and wake up in the middle of telling someone how unfair life is. That's okay; in fact you can consider this a second cue—the sudden realization that you've been reinjuring yourself. Once you see that, use the tool immediately.

People are especially prone to missing the first cue when something big and shocking happens, like getting fired out of the blue or finding out your spouse has been cheating on you. It's almost as if the jolt dislodges everything you've learned about handling injuries. But at the end of the day, it doesn't matter how you ended up in the repetitive hell of reinjury; what matters is that you use the Tower to get out of it as quickly as you can.

Don't relent. I had a patient who, at the reading of his father's will, found out he'd been disinherited. He had to use the Tower thirty times a day for a while. As the obsessive sense of injury lifted, he was eventually able to arrive at a more balanced view of his father's good and bad qualities.

The third use of the tool is as preparation for future injury. Often you know something is coming—like an event or a work presentation or a performance—where there is a risk of injury. Even if it's weeks before the intimidating event, use the tool each time anticipatory fear comes up. You imagine the injury, evoke the pain, and process it using the tool. As you use the tool preemptively, you'll find yourself much less afraid when the real event happens.

Finally, there are some people who need to use the tool as a daily practice, independent of what is happening in their lives. If your victimhood is long-standing and deeply ingrained, the Tower can become part of a comprehensive effort to change your personality.

This is an ambitious project, but it's fully possible for those who are determined. It requires you to use the Tower in a systematic way, every day, whether events require it or not. Pick two or three arbitrary times to practice the tool: perhaps when you get up in the morning and before you fall asleep at night, or maybe with each meal.

The secret to real personality change is to practice with

the most painful injury you can remember. You'll know you're changing when someone says or does something that would normally get you up in arms and it slides right off your back. No matter what conventional wisdom tells you, there's no limit to how deeply you can change yourself.

The Tower in Real Life

The Tower—if used conscientiously—can transform more that just an episode of hurt feelings. It can transform your whole inner being. In the ancient world, this inner transformation was initiated by a ritual baptism in water. The transformation of the modern person isn't a ritual, it's a real transformation, and the medium isn't water, it's pain.

You can't transform something until you accept it and take it inside yourself. The driving force of this transformation is the heart. The heart accepts whatever pain you are in and transmutes it. It transforms death into more life, and as you feel this "extra" life inside you, death becomes less intimidating.

This excess of life is the basis of courage—the feeling that you have more than enough life in you to overcome death in whatever form it takes, including criticism, failure, rejection, terror, etc. But thinking about it doesn't create more life; you need the Tower to unlock the heart's power in a way you can feel.

All this talk of death and life can get a little abstract. An everyday example of death that you're bound to experience is failure. We tend to quit after a failure because we can't handle any more of the hurt feelings it brings. Used diligently, the Tower keeps you moving forward no matter how many times you fail—this is how you conquer death. Andrew was a perfect example.

It was bad enough that Andrew wouldn't risk creating another segment after the first one failed, but when he blamed his mentor for not giving him a position he hadn't earned, he destroyed any chance of advancing his career. I told him this clearly, and after painful weeks of thinking about it he came into my office and said he wanted to make things right with his mentor.

"I want to apologize to him for acting like a babyish asshole."

I asked him why.

"He was right, I need to do another segment."

"What are you waiting for?"

"It's humiliating to eat it like that."

"That's a good thing." Before he could give me one of those are-you-nuts looks, I explained. "Humiliation is just another type of pain. If you really want to get your career back, you're going to have your feelings hurt a lot. Think of it as part of your job."

"Doesn't that mean I'm failing?"

"No. It means you don't understand what success is. Success isn't being acclaimed for your next segment; it's not even getting your own show. Success is a way of life."

I could see he didn't understand.

"The reason you can't commit to anything is because it hurts you too much if it fails. Success means putting everything on the line and, if it doesn't work out, doing it again. And again. No blaming. No excuses."

To live like that, Andrew needed to use the Tower extensively. His mentor was gracious, but cautious about how committed Andrew really was. I told Andrew he had nothing to prove to his mentor—he had to prove his dedication to himself. As he used the tool, one thing was immediately obvious to me: he'd stopped complaining and whining. His days as a victim were over. However his future turned out would be the result of his own efforts.

THE ASCENDING NATURE OF LIFE (CYCLING UP)

Injuries are part of life, whether we like it or not. Part X tries to resist that by getting you to think whatever is happening shouldn't be. This doesn't make the adversity go away; it prolongs it and turns you into a victim. The Tower works because it allows you to embrace adversity and keep moving forward.

The more willing you are to embrace the pain of injuries, the faster you will recover from them. It's inspiring to watch our patients' recovery time shrink from days to minutes and even seconds as they use the Tower. As this happens, they feel a sense of having been "reborn." They have more energy, feel more confident, and move through life with greater purpose.

Life doesn't move in a straight line. There are moments of pain and adversity in everyone's life. With each of these obstacles, we have the ability to connect to the Life Force and recover—these are cycles of death and rebirth. Here's how it works:

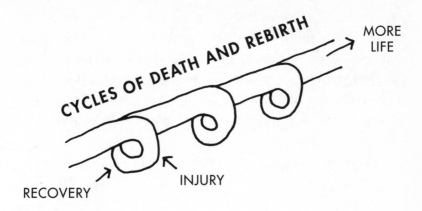

As you go through life, you get injured. Maybe your spouse cheats on you or your child lies about their grades or you get downsized in a company merger. Andrew was repeatedly injured in his professional life—his father rejected his career, he wasn't included in meetings, and his younger co-anchor got her own show before he did.

Whatever the injury, it sends you into a tailspin, which is represented by the line curving down in the picture. What happens at this point is critical. If you give in to Part X and rail against the injury, you'll become a victim and stay stuck in the "death" phase of the cycle, reinjuring yourself over and over again.

The Tower connects you to the Life Force, allowing the cycle to curve back up again. This rebirth fills you with a sense of aliveness and renewal, even in the most challenging situations. These cycles of death and rebirth are endless. They are the fundamental churning of life itself.

At first, most people don't like the idea that they're going to have to go through these cycles for the rest of their lives. But there's a tremendous reward that comes with embracing, and even looking forward to, these cycles. You gain an entirely new kind of confidence, a confidence that comes from knowing that although life will injure you, you'll always have access to the Life Force and its potential to overcome any obstacle you encounter.

Each time you go through the cycle of death and rebirth—whether large or small—you prove this to yourself. Each time you use the Tower, it pulls you out of death and into life. This is more than a concept; it's a reality that you can feel. It leaves you in a better place than you were before the injury. Your Life Force gets stronger as you conquer each obstacle, and the overall trajectory of your life is one of ascension.

THE FATHER

The ancient world had a more intuitive grasp of these cycles of death and rebirth, and of their connection to the Life Force, than we do today. They encoded their wisdom in myths—visionary images of heroes who accepted their fate and plunged deeply into death, only to be reborn with renewed powers. In these stories, fate was often represented by the Father.

The most enduring example of this is Jesus's story. The night before he was to be crucified, Jesus took a walk to pray alone in the garden at Gethsemane. He asked God to be spared his terrible fate, saying, "Father, please take this cup from me." With that plea, Jesus identifies the Father as the all-powerful author of fate. His next few words reveal what our relationship with the Father must be: "Not my will, but thine be done." Jesus acknowledges that the will of the Father governs everything that happens to us, and that our role is to *accept* this. In this acceptance is the potential of rebirth.

The Father is an archetype. He has nothing to do with your personal, human father. In the last chapter, we described the archetypal Mother as the cosmic force of love in the universe. The archetypal Father is the cosmic force of fate.

When you think of fate, you think of things that can't be avoided or that have a sense of inevitability. Time is a good example. If you're reading this at eight-thirty, in a half hour it's going to be nine o'clock, whether you like it or not. When you feel the inevitability of time passing, you're experiencing the Father. It's no coincidence that the personification of time is Father Time.

There are events in your life that are just as inevitable as the next thirty minutes going by. They come from the Father, and they can't be avoided. Many of these events are hurtful: you're in a marriage you think is going well, but out of nowhere, your spouse tells you he or she is unhappy; you put your heart and soul into a sales presentation for a client and they decide to go with a competitor. There are an infinite number of examples, some petty, others tragic. But, regardless of the scale, all these events have something in common: they're sent to you by the Father.

Even more important, once the Father sends an event into your life, it is irrevocable. If you look back at whatever happened to you in the past, it's now fixed; you can't go back and make it un-happen. Your opinion of it—whether you wish it hadn't happened or you blame yourself or someone else for it—doesn't matter. It is forever engraved in the past. This is important because *all* injuries happened in the past, even if they happened only a second ago. When you look back at an injury, whether it was yesterday or ten years ago, you are looking at the work of the Father.

Part X rebels against the terrible finality of this, but when you can admit that all injuries have one, ultimate source—the Father—it makes them much easier to accept. You can stop being a victim and obsessing about who injured you, why it happened, how unfair it was, etc., and shift your focus to recovery. The Father injured you, and the details don't matter. Your job is to grow from it.

But why does growth have to be so painful? The Father sees more potential for us than we see for ourselves—potential that comes from the pulsing Life Force inside each of us. But he also sees that much of the time we don't have access to that force. Part X has surrounded our heart with a hard shell of utter egotism. Just as the hard shell of a nut has to be cracked open to get to the meat inside, so must the Father shatter our hearts in order for us to experience that power. The injuries we face are a gift. They crack the shell around our heart and lead us to rediscover our Life Force and reach our full potential.

FREQUENTLY ASKED QUESTIONS

I've never thought of myself as a victim, so how does the Tower apply to me?

Most people don't like to think of themselves as "victims." But we're using the word to describe a state of mind that everyone falls into from time to time. It's a state of mind in which you're judging the injury ("It's unfair"), rather than getting over it. That doesn't help you recover; it actually hinders you. So no matter how you describe yourself, the Tower will help you recover faster from this state of mind.

I'm a writer and I've never had a manuscript accepted anywhere. It hurts, but it also makes me question whether I should keep writing or switch to something where I'd be more successful. Isn't there a point at which you should call it quits?

This is a big and difficult decision to make. What you don't want to do is quit something you may have great passion for because you can't deal with the pain. The first thing to do is use the Tower not to get some external result, but to get yourself out of the victim state. It's impossible to evaluate your talents when you're hurt. That means every injury needs to be processed immediately. Once you no longer feel demoralized, you can objectively look at whether you might change careers or not. If you do quit, you need to change careers with a sense of victory or strength, not because you've failed or you want to avoid future pain. It needs to be your decision, not Part X's.

I notice the drawing in this chapter is similar to the drawing in the Chapter 5, The Mother. What's the reason for that?

Cyclicity is built into the fabric of every problem described in the book. There are times when it's easier to fight your impulses and times when it's harder; there are times when you have more energy and times when you have less; there are times when your mood is up and times when it's down; and there are times when it's easy to handle injuries and times when it's more difficult. What we want to show you is how the tools can enable you to recover faster, which means that the overall quality of your life improves—it ascends. In a sense, the overall process is the same, but the specific challenges and skills are different in each chapter.

In your first book, The Tools, *you describe a state of mind called "the Maze." What's the difference between the Maze and the situation that the Tower addresses?*

Those who are stuck in the Maze are usually fixated on one particular offense or one person. They're obsessed, waiting for the other person to apologize or make amends. All your focus and attention is drawn to that person, and the only thing that will get you out of the Maze is the tool Active Love (see Appendix). In contrast, being a victim has to do with your relationship with the whole world. It's not just about one person who is inhabiting your mind, it's thinking that all of life is against you. Your life is kept small by fear. If you attempt to break out of that state, you'll have to go through fear, which will feel like a death. The process is deeper than getting out of the Maze, but it will develop a degree of courage that will change your relationship to life itself.

What is the light that permeates my heart when I'm in the Tower? Is that God?

This is a common question. What we have found is at the beginning it's better to answer that question in whatever way makes you most comfortable and helps you use the tool. There is a lot of variation possible with visualizations. You may prefer a warm or cool light, an intense or diffused light. There is no one way to do it. The best thing you can do is to go into this with an open mind and assume in the process your sense of what the light really is will develop through experience.

OTHER USES OF THE TOWER

> **THE TOWER INCREASES YOUR SELF-CONTROL.**
> When we get injured, we tend to act out, either to retaliate or to make ourselves feel better, or both. This can take the form of raging, eating, flirting, and so on. The Tower, because it enables us to process injuries quickly, also helps us contain the self-destructive behaviors.

Frank was a police officer in a tough neighborhood. He was known and well respected by almost everyone on his beat. He had grown up in a broken family and had been abused as a child. He walked around every day with a deep shame. Terrified that someone would find out his secret, he lived an isolated life. The only people he let in were the neighborhood teenagers. He was always available to give them the guidance no one had given him at their age.

As much as he was liked, most of those in his precinct avoided him. On several occasions, when someone asked him a question about himself, he was overcome with rage and had to walk away. The questions were innocent, but he misperceived them as accusations and judgments about his "strange" background. He'd replay these conversations over and over until they coalesced into a huge wound.

Not wanting to spend the rest of his life in emotional exile, he found the nerve to start therapy. The Tower was immensely helpful because it allowed him to be honest about what had happened to him and then use the tool immediately to keep his emotional pain at a tolerable level. In a slow but consistent process, he began to let go of his rage, no longer feeling like a victim of abuse that had happened twenty years before.

> **THE TOWER ENABLES YOU TO TAKE MORE CREATIVE AND INTERPERSONAL RISKS.** If you can't recover from injuries, you tend to shy away from taking risks. (By definition, what makes something risky is the chance that you could get injured.) Therefore, the Tower makes you better at the risks that lead to a full life.

Alice had been the assistant to a stockbroker for five years. Her boss was fast-talking, persuasive, well dressed, and well connected. But he was lazy. Alice was the opposite. She was organized, curious, and responsible—but not self-promotional. Her boss depended on her to keep up with the technical information that the research department turned out. He also relied on her to take clients' calls when he didn't want to be bothered, which was often.

The result was that she built up a huge body of invest-ment knowledge and close personal relationships with most of his clients. After a while, they preferred to speak to her rather than her boss. Because she was quiet and loyal, she didn't complain. After a number of years, she got up the nerve to ask him if he'd help her get into a training program for aspiring brokers.

He said no. Not wise to the ways of the world, she was shocked that he didn't recognize her potential. The real prob-lem was that he recognized her potential too well. He'd never get another assistant like her, and without her he'd actually have to do his job. He told her she needed several more years of seasoning before she could be considered for the pro-gram.

She couldn't get out of her mind the thought that if the shoe were on the other foot, she wouldn't have treated him that way. She was thrown into a world of hurt, and, having no idea how to get out of it, she started therapy. I told her she'd have to leave her job and get into a program on her own. She'd never taken that kind of risk in her life.

We started slowly, just using the Tower for practice. Then she used the tool to help her take small risks like con-necting to other aspiring brokers online. She got a bit bolder after that, standing up to her boss when she wanted vacation time and refusing to do things that were his responsibility, not hers. Finally, she used the tool to develop enough cour-age to quit. There was no way of knowing where that would take her, but she walked out knowing that if the world knocked down her confidence, she could regain it.

THE TOWER ALLOWS YOU TO GET ALONG WITH DIFFICULT PEOPLE. Everyone has someone in their life who's hurtful. If the person is peripheral, like an acquaintance, you can avoid them or get rid of them. But sometimes it's your kid, your father-in-law, a sibling, or someone close whom you can't stand but are stuck with. The Tower, by enabling you to recover from injuries faster, allows you to be with the person and nullify their impact on you.

Bruce was the CEO of a large manufacturing company with several thousand employees. He was tough, decisive, and had a very clear idea of what he wanted from each and every employee. At work, he was fair and consistent, but with his wife he had "no voice." She would speak over him, interrupt him, and make faces while he tried to express himself. She wouldn't shut him down when there were others around; at those moments, there was a show of marital harmony. But that would end the moment they were alone again.

He was accustomed to conflict in the business world, and he could call up a great deal of aggression when he needed to. But he'd been raised in a family where there was constant emotional and physical warfare, and he vowed not to have that energy in his home, especially after they had children. He took his role as the keeper of the peace seriously, and his wife, knowing that, would provoke him every chance she got, daring him to lose control and destroy any sense of peace.

Not knowing how to put a stop to her torture without

becoming warlike put him in a catch-22 situation. If he couldn't stop her, he felt inadequate as a parent and as a man; if he attacked back, he was allowing conflict to poison the family, making him a failure as a peacekeeper. The only answer was to use the Tower both during and after her attacks. Paradoxically, each time he transformed his hurt feelings using the tools, he felt a sense of confidence that didn't depend on influencing his wife's behavior.

SUMMARY

HOW PART X ATTACKS YOU: *When someone hurts or wrongs you, X floods you with injured feelings that are so strong you can't remain open or vulnerable; you can no longer give life your all. It keeps the injured feelings alive through "reinjury."*

HOW THIS DEADENS YOU: *If you don't know how to recover from injuries, you can't take the emotional and creative risks that are essential to living a full life. Instead of being fully alive, you get Part X's booby prize: the self-righteous certainty that whatever happened shouldn't have happened. You lose relationships and opportunities, and live a timid life.*

HOW PART X TRICKS YOU INTO GIVING IN: *It convinces you, on an unconscious level, that you are "special." You are above the indignities that are part of everyday life. Essentially, it positions each injury as a kind* *of "death," a final end point from which you can't recover. When you do get injured (which is inevitable), it convinces you that you're special in another way by telling you the whole universe is against you. You become a victim.*

THE SOLUTION: *The Tower forces you to die an emotional death and accept all the hurt feelings into your heart. Your heart has the power to be reborn and participate in life without having to be special or "right."*

Chapter Seven

Truth, Beauty, and Goodness

Every time Part X drags you into a hole and you
use tools to climb out, you complete a cycle—
and with each cycle you grow and become more
fully alive. In this chapter, Barry shows you the
transformative results: you discover Truth,
Beauty, and Goodness—forces that guide you in
the ascent to your highest potential.

At first, when you use the tools, you'll sim-
ply be grateful to get past the old habits that have held you
back for so long. You're sticking to a budget after years of
impulsive spending. You're working on a project in the eve-
nings, when you've always needed to veg out. A venture you
set your hopes on fails, and instead of getting depressed, you
pick yourself up and move on to something even better.
Someone has always been critical of you, but now, instead of
taking it to heart, you're able to shrug it off.

This doesn't mean the problems won't recur. Part X
never stops attacking you, and it will drag you back into a

hole: you'll cheat on your diet, give in to your kids because you're too tired to oppose them, allow a setback to defeat you, etc. But by using the tools, you'll climb out of the hole. Each time you complete one of these cycles, your Life Force grows. You might not notice the effects immediately, but you shouldn't expect to. You wouldn't lift weights and expect your physique to magically improve in a week, but if you keep at it, your body will change. The tools require the same persistence, but when you use them continuously it isn't your body that changes—it's your whole life that expands.

It's hard to have faith in this. By the time we reach adulthood, Part X has successfully diminished our dreams of what life could be like; we're habituated to a watered-down version of what's possible. But the more persistently you fight Part X, the more you feel the bracing winds of life's limitless potential. Your problems no longer stop you—they energize you to work even harder for your aspirations.

As the dark cloud of impossibility lifts, even more profound and mysterious changes occur. It's no exaggeration to say that when your Life Force increases, *everything* changes—even how you see yourself and the world around you. To understand why this happens, we have to delve into one of the deepest mysteries of life.

What we're casually calling the Life Force is an incomprehensible, forceful intelligence that's almost impossible to describe. Compared to it, we are like single drops of seawater trying to understand how the ocean works—its tides, currents, waves, temperature, etc. It's beyond our reckoning.

But in a sense, the Life Force tries to help us understand it better. It presents itself in three simplified forms: Truth,

Beauty, and Goodness. Philosophers call these "transcendentals"—eternal, unchanging principles that organize all of existence. In the same way the Father, Son, and Holy Spirit represent the Christian God, Truth, Beauty, and Goodness represent different aspects of the Life Force.

If you've heard of these principles at all, it was most likely when you were trying to stay awake in philosophy class your freshman year in college. That's where I learned them—and promptly dismissed them because they weren't relevant to my highest priority that year: I *really* wanted a girlfriend. (And I had enough sense to know that working Truth, Beauty, and Goodness into a pickup line would forever brand me as a nerd.) But it wouldn't have mattered even if I had been interested in these principles. In academia, Truth, Beauty, and Goodness are presented as dry, abstract concepts.

It was only later in my life, when I started to use the tools consistently and my Life Force increased, that I began to experience Truth, Beauty, and Goodness as real forces that made life meaningful. They began to give me something I'd never had before: a sense that I was living for something greater than myself. These *ideas* became *ideals*—something worth living for.

You've probably felt these forces without identifying them as such—everyone has. But we want you to experience their presence in a more consistent way so that they become your North Star—a guide to your life. Each one assists you in a specific way. Truth *reveals* Part X, exposing all the ways it has lied to you. Beauty *inspires* you to fight X, by giving you glimpses of how wondrous the world would be without it. And Goodness embraces the negative energy of X and *transforms* it into virtue. To put it simply, Truth reveals your path, Beauty inspires you to walk it, and Goodness enables you to spread virtue along the way. It is on this path that you gain the greatest reward: you know who you are and why you are here. Your soul finds its true place in the universe.

But there's a catch. By now, you should know that if Truth, Beauty, and Goodness are the life-changing forces I've described, Part X will do everything it can to cut you off from them. The way it does this is by creating a false version of each and convincing you it's the real thing. Part X's substitutes aren't even forces—they're just empty concepts. (I'll refer to them in lowercase, as truth, beauty, and goodness.) A force gets inside of you and *moves* you; it expands, inspires, and rouses you to action. A concept does none of these things. Your head understands concepts, but your heart is untouched by them. So when Part X directs you to the fake versions, you feel nothing. There you are, bored in philosophy class, unaware that you've missed an encounter with otherworldly powers that could give you the life you've always wanted.

Anyone can tap into these powers. But you have to start with something that's easier said than done: you have to stop lying.

WELCOME TO THE LIARS' CLUB

You're a liar.

Don't be offended—I'm a liar too; everyone is. That's right . . . everyone lies, especially to themselves.

If you need proof, just look at the myriad New Year's resolutions you've made: "This year I'm going to live a healthier lifestyle, spend more time with friends and family, save more and spend less," etc. If you haven't kept them (and most of us drop them before the end of January), then you've lied to yourself.

But lies don't just happen at New Year's. You've seen numerous examples in the last four chapters: You tell yourself "I need a drink" at the end of a long day, when the truth is you'd be better off without one. You say you're too tired to play with your kids, when the truth is it would *give* you energy. You're convinced you'll never find another relationship, when the truth is you've lost perspective. Your boss promotes a rival and you tell yourself, "It's not fair," when fairness isn't the issue—it just hurts.

You know who perpetuates these lies: Part X. Lies are one of the best methods X employs to keep you stuck in a repetitive rut. That's why it got Marty to deny his lack of self-control, convinced Beth her naps were indispensable, set Ann on a wild-goose chase to find the perfect guy, and convinced Andrew he was a victim. Each lie you tell yourself is like a silken thread in what becomes a web of deceit— immobilizing you while Part X drains your Life Force. If you're serious about fulfilling your potential, you must face these lies and break free of them.

It seems like that should be simple. All you need to do is start telling yourself the truth, and presto—you're released from Part X. But is knowing the truth really enough to activate its life-changing power? Clearly not: everyone knows what's required to live a healthy life—a good night's sleep, consistent exercise, and a healthy diet—yet for most people, simply telling themselves that isn't enough. That's because even after you know the truth, Part X has a way of neutralizing its power. It creates a false version of the truth—stripped of its ability to change your life. You can know it in your head without ever acting on it.

A patient of mine learned this the hard way. From an early age, Sheryl took care of her alcoholic mother. In a mother-daughter role reversal, every night she would rouse her mother from an intoxicated stupor, get her washed up, and tuck her into bed. The next morning, she'd charm her mom's boss into forgiving her tardiness and then get herself to school.

It wasn't an ideal childhood, but the effects on Sheryl weren't all bad. She learned to take responsibility for herself early in life, running a successful cosmetics line and, by age thirty, guiding a start-up through a successful public offering. But she also remained overinvolved in her mother's life, constantly pushing her into therapy, twelve-step groups, and treatment programs. Her mother dutifully attended them all, but there was never any real change—just an endless cycle. Sheryl would cajole her mother to get sober, and her mother would go on the wagon. Then she would relapse, and Sheryl would go on an angry rampage. Her mother would apologize, Sheryl would forgive her, and the whole cycle would start up again.

Why would an intelligent, successful woman put herself through this futile cycle again and again? Deep down, Part X had convinced her she had the power to turn her mother into a responsible, sober adult.

Fortunately, Sheryl had a group of close friends who put

together a makeshift "intervention." They told her the truth: "Your efforts are being wasted, and in the meantime, you have no life—when's the last time you went out on a date?" At first, Sheryl fought them, but eventually she realized she was doing too much; her mother had to choose sobriety for herself. The intervention helped Sheryl accept the truth: she was powerless to cure her mother's alcoholism.

You'd think that would be the end of the story. Now that she had admitted she was powerless, she'd stop trying to cure her mother, right?

Wrong. Part X has an amazing ability to get us to keep living a lie even after we've admitted the truth. It lies in wait for the right opportunity, which in Sheryl's case appeared when a work colleague told her about a new rehab in Malibu that had helped her son. Its upbeat, non-shaming philosophy, matched by accommodations rivaling a luxury hotel, were a quantum leap above any recovery program Sheryl's mother had enrolled in. But Sheryl had admitted that she was powerless; how could she justify recommending the rehab to her mother? Part X found an easy rationalization: "You haven't bugged your mother about her drinking for months. And this is an exceptional program. How are you going to feel if your mom dies of alcoholism because you refused to let her know about something that could have saved her?"

That was persuasive. But it's one thing to lie to yourself; it's another to lie to a group of people who might accuse you of backsliding. So when Sheryl met with her friends, she came on strong, looking each one in the eye and reiterating that she accepted her powerlessness. "All I want to do is hand her the rehab brochure and walk away—she can throw it in

the trash for all I care." It was a compelling performance—
the kind you put on when you're trying to convince yourself
as much as the people around you. Her friends agreed and
her mother checked in the very next day.

Sure enough, two weeks later, Sheryl got a call from the
rehab. Her mother had disappeared from the facility and gone
on a bender. This time, Sheryl didn't get angry, she got depressed. That's when a friend referred her to me. She was
feeling listless and morose. "I just don't see the point of anything anymore. I feel dead inside."

I told her the deadness was something she could recover
from, and taught her the Mother tool. My immediate aim
was for the tool to help her bounce back from her mother's
relapse. But long-term, I hoped it would give her a more profound experience of the Truth. She'd *admitted* she was powerless, but she hadn't *experienced* it.

Sheryl began to feel more alive, and over time, the Mother
became increasingly real to her. About a month later, she arrived at my office and handed me her journal. Something so
momentous had happened she'd felt compelled to write it
down.

> *I was climbing into bed and remembered to use the
> Mother tool. But the moment I closed my eyes it felt
> different—the Mother was actually in the room with me,
> not just in my imagination. Gradually, she took charge and
> guided me through a visualization so vivid it felt real.*
>
> *I was a child, in the shabby apartment I grew up in,
> bombarded with old sensations: the rancid smell of booze
> and puke, the ghostly light of the TV bouncing off the*

walls, Mom slouching bleary-eyed on the couch, a bottle of gin at her breast. It struck me how tenderly she was holding it—like an infant.

I blurted out, "Why don't you ever hold me that way?" I tried to pry the bottle away from her but she was too strong. Her face was twisted into a mask of vicious hatred. She'd never looked that way before and it terrified me. She got up abruptly and walked away. I ran after her, begging, "Don't leave me alone!" But she acted like I didn't exist. She left, the door banging shut with finality. She was gone. I was alone. And that's when it hit me: I've ALWAYS been alone. I began to cry . . . convulsive sobs coming from a place I never knew existed.

Something told me to use the Mother tool again. She came to me immediately, infinite waves of loving warmth embracing me, lifting me out of the pit. She stayed with me and the grief gradually subsided. When I looked into her eyes, I saw something new: she was proud of me for facing the truth. My mother loves alcohol more than she loves me. She always has. And I have to stop fighting it.

WHICH VERSION IS IT?

Part X will do everything it can to prevent you from experiencing the Truth. Its first tactic is obvious—it gets you to lie to yourself. Sheryl simply refused to accept that it was impossible to change her mother despite decades of trying and failing. But even after you face the truth, Part X has a more subtle, clever tactic. It creates a false version of the truth—drained of all its power. It gets you to believe that the truth is abstract—just words in your head. So once Sheryl came to the realization "I am powerless," she thought she was done. She felt virtuous admitting something she'd never admitted before—but it didn't change anything.

To free herself, Sheryl had to experience the Truth in a new way. She used the Mother tool to accomplish this, but all the tools in this book (and our first book) will lead you to a new experience of the Truth. No longer an impotent thought that makes no difference in your life, the Truth becomes an irresistible force that blazes through your soul. The Truth is a *revelatory* force—it shines a light on Part X's darkest machinations. Its revelatory power enables you to expand your life in ways you never thought possible.

To live in alignment with the Truth, you need to be able to differentiate it from its false substitute. The following three principles show you how to make this distinction. You'll begin to *live* the Truth, instead of talking about it.

PRINCIPLE 1: THE TRUTH IS A FORCE, NOT A THOUGHT

When you use the tools enough times, the Truth *hits* you the way a force does. That's why we say, "I was *struck* by the truth." The false version, because it's just words, is stripped of this dynamism. That's how Sheryl was able to declare herself powerless and then do a U-turn and pack her mother off to another rehab. All Part X had to do was replace one truth—"I'm powerless" with another truth—"I'd be a terrible daughter if I withheld life-saving information from my mother." It wasn't until she used the Mother tool repeatedly that the Truth *hit* her, and she was able break the old habit.

Don't misunderstand: it's better to admit the truth than to deceive yourself. "I just lost my temper and said something hurtful." "I've lost perspective—things are not as bad as they seem." "Getting high tonight is going to feel good but it'll hurt me in the long run." But Part X wants you to believe that your life will change merely by thinking these truths. It won't. The fake version of truth is safe, removed, academic, because it occurs only in your head. The Truth—as a force—thunders through your entire being. It has a life of its own. The great American novelist David Foster Wallace expressed it beautifully: "The truth will set you free. But not until it is finished with you."

PRINCIPLE 2: THE TRUTH HURTS

It's painful to be seized by this otherworldly force. In fact, we tell our patients, "If it doesn't hurt, you're probably lying to yourself."

The Truth is merciless, holding up a mirror that shows you who you are without regard to who you *wish* you were. You wanted to do something special with your life and you're not doing it. You vowed not to make the mistakes your parents made—and you're making them with your children. People say you have a problem and deep down you know they're right, but you keep denying it. The Truth forces your identity to expand, encompassing the bad as well as the good.

The Truth is also painful because it unmasks the lies other people have told you. Sheryl's mother had always presented herself as a harmless old woman whose only sin was never getting her life together. The Truth revealed a much darker side. Underneath the hapless alcoholic was an exploitive parent who loved booze more than the young daughter who had needed her. She had forced Sheryl to shoulder responsibilities no child should be burdened with, and now she was manipulating the adult Sheryl—making just enough of an effort at sobriety to keep Sheryl's hopes alive and the gravy train going. Only the revelatory power of Truth allowed Sheryl to glimpse her mother's Part X, a parasitic part of her that would have happily sucked the life out of her own daughter. This was painful, but without it, Sheryl would never have been able to set the limits she needed to set.

You must accept the pain of whatever Truths you're avoiding in your own life. This exercise will give you a preview of the kind of pain you're in for, so you'll be prepared to handle it:

- Think about an area of life where you might be lying to yourself. Maybe you've promised to do something and you keep putting it off. Maybe you put all the blame on the other person whenever you have a fight with them. Maybe you've deluded yourself into believing someone close to you (spouse, friend, etc.) was working on himself when in fact he's not.
- Now close your eyes and imagine accepting the Truth. You have failed yourself and others by not delivering on your promises. You've failed to take responsibility for your part in escalating rather

than diminishing conflict between you and someone else. Your spouse is not working on himself—
he's stuck.
- Don't minimize or run away from this Truth. Instead, face it; let it sink in. What does it feel like?

The pain you just experienced is nothing compared to
what you'll feel when the Truth—a force with a mind of its
own—burns through you. We rarely feel this pain, because
human beings are naturally lazy and pain-avoidant. We want
our truths served to us without the anguish that results from
living a lie. This is another reason Part X's version of truth
is so tempting: it's painless. You think it . . . and you're done.

There's a name for the spontaneous upwelling of pain
that occurs when you allow the Truth to rip you open. Traditional psychology calls it a "catharsis." Grief, terror, rage,
etc., are all part of the experience. Most psychotherapists
focus on these powerful emotions, thinking that it's simply
the release of them that's healing. It isn't. The ancient Greeks
had a deeper appreciation for what a catharsis was. To them,
it connoted a process in which you are purified. What are you
being purged of? The lies with which Part X has limited
your life. Imagine it: For a moment, you are free, honest,
completely clean with yourself. The Truth—an eternal, im-
mutable, and unstoppable fire—has burned through all the
lies. In this moment of freedom from Part X, you can fulfill
the highest mandate of the ancient world: to "know thy-
self"—as the flawed, limited being you are, and as the pure
potential being you could become. You are reborn.

This changes you as a person. You get a glimpse of everything you could be if you lived your life in complete alignment with the Truth. You also see—with stark clarity—the ways you've fallen short of that. Most important, you know, deep inside, that the choice—freedom or enslavement—is yours, moment to moment, for the rest of your life.

PRINCIPLE 3: TRUTH REQUIRES ONGOING ACTION

There's one more way you can differentiate the Truth from Part X's false version. The fake version is a one-time thing—you say it ("I'm powerless") and you're done. But for the Truth to be real, it has to become an ongoing practice.

There's no getting rid of Part X, and it's not going to stop convincing you to lie to yourself just because you've had a painful revelation. Sheryl, for example, had to continue to fight the urge to rescue her mother. And she had to expand the revelation she had with her mother to all her relationships, where she discovered the same pattern of taking too much responsibility for others. Adherence to the Truth had to become a way of life with her.

For you to do the same, you'll have to convert "armchair" truths into action steps in the real world. If you do this, you'll feel a sense of integrity you've never experienced before. Try this exercise:

- Go back to the personal Truth you identified in the last exercise. You've failed to deliver on your promises. You've denied responsibility for your role in conflicts. Someone close to you says he's working on himself, but really isn't.

- Identify a few specific action steps you could take that would be consistent with that Truth. You could fulfill one of the promises you've made right now. You could apologize to someone you've fought with. You might tell the person who says he's trying to change that you're beginning to feel hopeless it'll ever happen.

- Now imagine taking those steps, and others as they occur to you, as the weeks, months, and years stretch into the future. Imagine doing whatever it takes to live in alignment with the Truth, over a long period of time. See if you get an intimation of the kind of person you become. Focus on how you'd be different on the inside, rather than how your outer circumstances would change. What would it feel like to be this new "you"?

This is the "you" who can live in alignment with the Truth for the rest of your life—in service to something greater than yourself. There's something magical about that. Most of us live for ourselves—narrowly focusing on our immediate needs and petty fears. But when you dedicate yourself to the Truth, you align yourself with something more expansive—a force that existed before you were born and will continue after you pass away. Life has meaning when you dedicate it to something more than yourself.

You'll also experience a burst of energy you've never felt before. You may not realize it, but it's exhausting to fight the Truth—a force with otherworldly power. Before her epiphany, Sheryl was always so drained by her mother that she had abandoned her own romantic life. Once you surrender to the Truth, all of the energy you wasted trying to reject it becomes available for you; you feel motivated to expand your life.

None of this means that Part X will stop trying to get you to lie to yourself. But the stronger your relationship with the Truth is, the more easily you'll be able to see through those lies. In fact, many of our patients reach the point where they look forward to catching Part X in the act of lying. They know that whatever the lie is, there's a life-expanding Truth waiting to be uncovered underneath.

We don't want to make this sound easy: these rewards are available only for those with the stamina to withstand the pain of exposing their own lies, and to make the ongoing effort to act in accordance with the Truth. But fortunately, the Life Force provides us with a source of motivation to do the work; its vehicle is Beauty.

WATER, WATER, EVERYWHERE AND NOT A DROP TO DRINK

Her blond hair undulating in a soft, slow-motion breeze, a young woman stares at you seductively. She is loveliness personified—perfect, unblemished skin, penetrating blue eyes, and a voice that melts like butter. If you're a woman, she's promising you can *be* her; if you're a man, she's promising you can *have* her. For a second, you're swept into believing that if you buy what she's selling (for an "incredibly low price"), it can happen!

Images of beauty bombard us continually—on billboards,

television, magazine covers, and movies. Given how obsessed we are with beauty, you'd think we'd be able to see it in ourselves and the world around us. But how often do you look at yourself in the mirror and admire what you see? How often are you struck with the beauty of your surroundings? Most people are cut off—even if they see it, it doesn't affect them in any permanent way.

What's going on? We're barraged with images of beauty—and yet they fail to inspire us in the way they could. The simple answer is that we look for it only on the surface of things. A beautiful woman is young, curvaceous, and willowy. A handsome man is angular, chiseled, and muscular. But to appreciate the universality of beauty, we have to look deeper. You've probably had moments when you saw beauty in something that appeared ordinary or even ugly on the surface. These experiences teach us something important: real beauty shimmers underneath the surface of everything.

WHAT IS BEAUTY?

In the movie *American Beauty*, a young videographer asks the girl he's falling in love with, "Do you want to see the most beautiful thing I've ever filmed?" She nods and he flicks on a video. The camera follows a discarded plastic bag as it whirls in the breeze in front of a dull redbrick wall; the ground is strewn with dead leaves. The scene is so mundane you wouldn't normally notice it, and yet you sense something else there. In voice-over, the young man narrates: "It was one of those days . . . when it's a minute away from snowing. And there's this electricity in the air. You can almost hear it, right?

And this bag was just . . . dancing with me. Like a little kid begging me to play with it." Suddenly you realize that what is commonplace on the surface has a kind of indefinable beauty underneath it. He continues his narration: "That's the day I realized there was this entire life behind things . . . and this incredibly benevolent force wanted me to know that there was no reason to be afraid . . . ever."

That's what Beauty is: *the Life Force peeking out from behind the surface of the ordinary world.* In this book, we've already described the Life Force inside you. But the Life Force is also *outside* you. It animates people and inhabits objects—buildings, streets, railroads, telephone poles, etc. The Life Force inside these things is what provides them with real Beauty. If you can perceive it, even something that appears ugly on the surface can come to life and inspire you. If you can't perceive it, you're cut off from a powerful ally in your fight against Part X.

Beauty is bountiful and ever present, which is why the videographer found it such a source of reassurance. Part X has conditioned us to perceive beauty as confined to certain places or people, but it isn't—it's everywhere. Shimmering underneath the surface of everything, Beauty makes even ordinary things sparkle with life—a plastic bag dancing in the wind, the weather-beaten face of someone who's lived a long, full life, a street blighted with billboards and trash. Like Truth, Beauty is an autonomous force—it comes from beyond and has the potential to break you open and change your life.

WHY BEAUTY MATTERS

It's obvious to most people why the Truth is important. But why should we care about Beauty—why does it matter? Beauty provides us with something we can't get anywhere else: the inspiration to fight as hard as we can against Part X. The enemy's most powerful weapon is the sense of impossibility it creates: it seems impossible to resist temptation, overcome obstacles, meet life's demands, and so on. This constant thrumming—"Give up, you can't, it's impossible"—destroys our dreams and aspirations before we even act on them.

That's why Beauty is so important. By revealing an entire dimension of life that's *untouched* by Part X, Beauty pierces through the miasma of impossibility like a ray of sunlight, injecting you with the sense that everything is possible. Beauty inspires you to live a life that says "I can" rather than "I can't."

Beauty touches everyone's life differently. It allowed the videographer to overcome his fears. It will inspire you in a way that's unique to you. But I've never met anyone who hasn't felt Beauty free them from their limitations—if only momentarily. Hearing the rhythms and harmonies of a particular song can impel you to exercise harder and longer than normal. The jubilation of a child's laughter can awaken you from the doldrums. An unusually vivid sunset can motivate you to express yourself creatively.

Beauty is a unique resource in the fight against Part X because it's *everywhere*; you can tap into it wherever you are. Moreover, it's available to everyone—rich, poor, deserving, undeserving, educated, uneducated. Like God's grace, it is *given*, not earned or purchased. And you never have to worry about running out of it, because it's infinite—it has never been depleted and never will be. Infinitely benevolent, Beauty never stops giving of itself.

One of the ways Part X gets us to believe that Beauty *doesn't* matter is by convincing us that life is all about just getting by—as if we're barely surviving. Beauty seems frivolous in a world where you could die at any moment. But it isn't—it never has been. Even in prehistoric times, when humankind was preoccupied with survival, people adorned their caves with paintings. Flutes have been discovered dating back to forty thousand years before Christ.

Even in modern times, people whose survival was at risk have relied on Beauty's inspirational force. One of the most striking examples of this appears in *Man's Search for Meaning*, Viktor Frankl's account of his imprisonment in Nazi concentration camps. In the camps, there was an ever-present threat of being shot, gassed, or hanged, but without running water, sanitation, or adequate nutrition, you were also likely to wither away slowly, through starvation, disease, overwork, or exhaustion. Yet for Frankl, it was the very bleakness of his surroundings that impelled him to find, in Beauty, a power that sustained him.

> *Another time we were at work in a trench. The dawn was grey around us; grey was the sky above; grey the snow in the pale light of dawn; grey the rags in which my fellow prisoners were clad, and grey their faces. I was again conversing silently with my wife, or perhaps I was struggling*

*to find the reason for my sufferings, my slow dying. In a
last violent protest against the hopelessness of imminent
death, I sensed my spirit piercing through the enveloping
gloom. I felt it transcend that hopeless, meaningless world,
and from somewhere I heard a victorious "Yes" in answer
to my question of the existence of an ultimate purpose. At
that moment a light was lit in a distant farmhouse, which
stood on the horizon as if painted there, in the midst of
the miserable grey of a dawning morning in Bavaria.*
"Et lux in tenebris lucent"—*and the light shineth in the
darkness.*

If Viktor Frankl was able to see Beauty piercing through
the bleakness of a Nazi concentration camp, it must indeed be
everywhere, available at all times. Beauty is like the air surrounding you; you can breathe it in whenever you need to.

THE ATTACK ON BEAUTY

So how does Part X stop you from doing that? As with
Truth, it substitutes a false version for the real thing. Whereas
Beauty is infinite—available to all people at all times—the
false version is finite, available only to an elite few. And because it's finite, the false version inspires only competition;
the conquest and ownership of it becomes the currency by
which we measure our status. If a guy sees a beautiful woman,
it isn't enough to admire her—he has to "have" her, and feels
threatened if she flirts with someone else. For the rich, it's
not enough to appreciate a Picasso, you must acquire one to
get a leg up on those who can't afford it. Even the beauty of

nature can be used for self-aggrandizement: it isn't enough to be awed by the magnificence of Mount Everest; an unprecedented number of climbers are possessed by the egotistical drive to "conquer" it.

But wait a minute. If Beauty is everywhere—available to everyone at all times—then who cares if someone else climbs Everest, buys a Picasso, or shows up at a party with a stunning companion? Why not be happy for them and go on admiring that beautiful plastic bag dancing in the breeze?

Getting us to compete for Beauty when it's infinitely available requires Part X to perpetrate a mass delusion. Remember that Beauty is part of the Life Force—a diffuse, intangible energy shimmering underneath the surface of everything. Trying to possess it is unthinkable; like grabbing a fistful of water, it would slip through your fingers. So X convinces you that the Life Force isn't everywhere, but, rather, centralized in certain objects—a stunning actress, a luxury car, an expensive home with a view, etc. Then it convinces you these objects are "beautiful" (and worth possessing), while others (like the plastic bag) have no value at all.

And X doesn't stop there. It strengthens this mass delusion by providing us with a standardized metric for determining which things are beautiful and which are not: a woman is beautiful if she's young, skinny, and has an unblemished, symmetrical face. A work of art is beautiful if buyers are willing to pay top dollar for it. If Part X can get all of us to agree to these standards, it's difficult to see Beauty in things that don't live up to them.

Worse, we regard these criteria as absolute—standing

for all time—when in reality, they're constantly changing. Judging by Cleopatra, big noses were all the rage in the ancient world—not so much anymore. There are societies where being fat is considered attractive (especially poor countries, where it's a sign of prosperity). Van Gogh made very little money from his paintings in his lifetime; now they sell for hundreds of millions of dollars. The paintings haven't changed—our standards of beauty have.

If the metrics we use to measure beauty are ever changing, then even if you attain the false version of beauty today, it will slip away from you tomorrow. And the equating of youth with beauty *guarantees* a futile quest for the fountain of youth. Whipped by the need to keep up appearances, we spend billions of dollars ($11 billion in 2012 alone) on cosmetic surgical procedures that are medically unnecessary. Millions of people cutting into their flesh, hoping to achieve the unattainable—and failing in the end. It's the demonic coup de grâce: we unleash the ugliest part of ourselves in the pursuit of Beauty—something that's already there in abundance.

It's time to accept the truth. Beauty cannot be captured, owned, or possessed. It's just the opposite: the mission of Beauty is to find *you*, open your heart, and inject it with the inspiration to fight Part X. If you allow that, you'll find yourself spreading the seeds of Beauty to everything and everyone around you.

As in the case of Truth, there are three principles that will help you differentiate true Beauty from Part X's false substitute. If you live according to these principles, you won't have to travel to a tropical paradise, have cosmetic surgery, or buy expensive clothes to find Beauty. You'll see it inside yourself and surrounding you in daily life.

PRINCIPLE 1: BEAUTY CAN ONLY BE SEEN BY THE HEART

Confucius, the ancient Chinese philosopher, said, "Everything has Beauty, but not everyone sees it." How can we train ourselves to perceive the Beauty around us? We have to stop looking only at the surface of things. Real Beauty moves surreptitiously *underneath* the surface of the visible world. To learn about something visible, you use intellectual tools. With a couch, for example, you can measure its length, analyze the way it's upholstered, make calculations to figure out if it will fit in your living room, etc. You do all this with your head.

Beauty is different. The only way to know it is by the awe it inspires in your heart. The heart can do what the head can't do: penetrate the surface and perceive the Beauty of the world moving invisibly beneath it. Michelangelo, one of the greatest sculptors of the Italian Renaissance, is said to have described his creative process this way: "I saw the Angel in the marble and carved until I set him free." In his heart, he saw the Beauty *within* the block of marble and kept carving until it was free of everything that didn't belong. We must do the same: use our hearts to look beneath the surface of ordinary objects and free the angel of Beauty residing in them.

You may not think you know how to see Beauty with

your heart, but you do. In childhood—before Part X took control of your perception—you saw everything with your heart. I remember this from my own childhood. I grew up in a lower-middle-class neighborhood, and yet almost every day the Beauty of the world bombarded my senses like a spraying hydrant on a hot summer day. I found it mesmerizing: the sun warming the dew, the breeze whispering through the trees, everything swaying in perfect harmony.

In adulthood, Part X moves the center of perception from the heart to the head. As a result, I now live in nicer surroundings, yet I struggle to see Beauty anywhere! I walk out my front door focused on where I'm going and what needs to be done when I get there. If I notice anything, my concerns are purely practical—the leaves need raking, another car is blocking mine, someone tipped over a trash can, etc. That's all Part X wants me to see.

Because children see with their hearts, they derive the benefits of Beauty: they have more energy, play with abandon, and often adapt to changes more quickly (and with fewer complaints) than adults. Without knowing it, they are inspired by the Beauty surrounding them. Any adult can recover these childhood abilities. Try this exercise:

- Close your eyes and go back to your childhood. Pick out someone or something that seemed beautiful at the time. It might have been a stuffed animal, a member of your family, or something less personal, like the sound of rain. Whatever you choose, focus on it until it drowns out everything else.

- Now imagine the same thing from an adult's point of view. How are the two perspectives different? Which perspective inspires you to fight Part X?

Adults see things with their heads. That vantage point screens out the aesthetic, narrowly focusing on the practical: "The stuffing is coming out of the teddy bear," "Every family member is overweight," "The rain reminds me that the roof might leak." That's how Part X nullifies the power of Beauty.

Traditional psychology puts a lot of emphasis on childhood to explain the origin of your problems. But to me the great value of early life is that it helps you remember a time when you looked at the world through a different pair of eyes—and reveled in the Beauty around you.

PRINCIPLE 2: BEAUTY HURTS

Part X's ability to blind us to the Beauty that surrounds us is abetted by a great ally: pain. It actually hurts to perceive the Beauty of the world around you. The pain can be sweet and liberating, but it hurts nonetheless. In *American Beauty*, the narrator ends his soliloquy this way: "Sometimes there's so much beauty in the world I feel like I can't take it. And my heart ... it's just going to cave in." Most of us are so pain-avoidant we sacrifice Beauty's inspiring power, living in a purely functional world.

Why does it hurt to take in something as salutary as Beauty? Beauty is life—when it enters you, it forces your heart to expand beyond where it's been before. Just like a physical muscle stretching past its normal limits, that hurts.

Unlike a physical muscle, however, your heart can expand without limit, encompassing more life than you've ever known. The writer Andrew Harvey put it this way: "If you're really listening, if you're awake to the poignant beauty of the world, your heart breaks regularly. In fact, your heart is made to break; its purpose is to burst open again and again so that it can hold evermore wonders."

These heartbreaking wonders make Beauty not only painful but scary. It's inevitable that Beauty will inspire you to take risks you wouldn't otherwise take. You may break out of your comfort zone and try something new—risk rejection by expressing love more passionately or risk failure by starting a new pet project. The heroes of ancient Greece risked their lives when their princess Helen—the beauty "that launched a thousand ships"—was kidnapped and abducted to Troy. It only makes sense that if Beauty can inspire you to risk more, Part X will use fear to stop you.

Obviously, Beauty isn't *only* about pain and fear; it can also fill you with intense delight. At some point, you've probably been entranced by a meteor blazing across the night sky, a song that sent your body swaying, or the grandeur of a summer thunderstorm. But Beauty is a force, and your encounters with it can also cause you to "come undone"—lose your composure. That's why we cry when we hear certain pieces of music or see certain films. The Santa Maria Nuova hospital in Florence, Italy, is accustomed to treating tourists who become dizzy and faint after gazing at Michelangelo's statue of David and other art treasures of the city. The same thing can happen when people are awed by natural beauty. Traditional psychology attributes this to a "psychosomatic" disorder (meaning it's all in your head), because it can't acknowledge that these people are actually responding to a force from beyond. But that's disrespectful—to the power of Beauty and to the human longing for its heart-expanding powers.

If it doesn't move, hurt, or scare you at least a little, you probably aren't dealing with the real version of Beauty. To experience these feelings, try this:

- Close your eyes and think of something you find beautiful. It might be a person, an inspired work of art or music, a shaft of light slicing through a dense forest, or anything else that has moved you with its beauty. Whatever it is, focus all of your attention on it.
- Now imagine that there's a powerful force—the force of pure Beauty—emanating from it. Feel the force approaching you, piercing your heart, and filling it with so much inspiration it feels like your heart could burst. Feel the pain. Relax, and let the force flow through you.

Think of the pain you just experienced as the price you pay for the inspiration you receive. If you're willing to pay the price, you'll receive the reward: your heart will expand, you'll fight harder against Part X, and you'll live an inspired life.

PRINCIPLE 3: BEAUTY IS AS BEAUTY DOES

There's a final way you can tell the difference between Beauty and Part X's false substitute. Real Beauty must be reflected in the way you live your life. To understand this, you must realize that there is a kind of Beauty reflected in things we don't normally assess in aesthetic terms. A relationship can be beautiful when two people weather many storms together and emerge loving and respectful of one another. Likewise, there are people who move through life with a kind of Beauty—handling difficult situations with delicacy and poise. When you react to someone's insults with forgiveness, when you show kindness to a stranger who's down on his luck, when you comfort someone who's grieving—you *personify* Beauty. In truth, every human endeavor has the potential to bring Beauty into the world. History is replete with examples; perhaps the most famous is Christ asking forgiveness for those who crucified him.

But there are modern examples as well. Lizzie Velásquez is a young woman who was born with an extremely rare congenital disease that, among other symptoms, prevents her from gaining weight. With her caved-in cheeks, stick-thin limbs, and off-kilter eyes, she is far from our modern notion of beauty. When she was seventeen years old, she stumbled across a YouTube video of herself titled "The World's Ugliest Woman," with thousands of comments like "Lizzie, please just do the world a favor, put a gun to your head and kill yourself." Rather than retaliate, Lizzie chose to respond with grace and nobility, reaching out to other victims of online bullying and eventually becoming a motivational speaker.

Essentially, her actions said, "I will take the ugliness you've thrown at me and use it to act with even greater Beauty."

Let's see how you might choose to act with Beauty. Think of someone who's so difficult they're able to get you to act in an ugly way. Try this exercise:

- Go back to the last exercise and reexperience the force of Beauty piercing your heart and filling you with inspiration.
- Place yourself in front of the difficult person and imagine them doing something provocative that would normally trigger the worst in you.
- Before you respond, reconnect to the flow of Beauty welling up inside your heart; use the other person's ugliness to strengthen, rather than weaken, your connection to it. If you were able to do this in real life, how would you respond differently to the other person?

When the ugliness of another person strengthens your inner commitment to Beauty, you've accomplished something profound. You've freed yourself from the noxious influence of another person. More important, you've solidified your connection to Beauty as a force. When you can align yourself with something greater than yourself—and remain true to it no matter the provocation—life becomes meaningful. You are dedicating yourself to something that transcends the pettiness of everyday life.

What this suggests is that Beauty can inspire us to be

better people. The reverse is also true—when you do the right thing, you bring more Beauty into the world. There is, in fact, an intimate connection between Beauty and Goodness—the third aspect of the Life Force. The ancient Greek word for Beauty—*kalos*—reflects this connection. The word can mean "beautiful," but it can also mean "praiseworthy."

There is a dynamic interplay between all three aspects of the Life Force, Truth, Beauty, and Goodness. As you've seen, Truth reveals Part X to you. Beauty inspires you to fight it. And when you fight the inner enemy, Goodness enters you and elevates everyone around you.

GOODNESS PERSONIFIED

Imagine this: It's 1960 and you are a leader of the civil rights movement. You're in Nashville, Tennessee, with a group of black student activists staging a protest at a "whites only" movie theater. You've spent hours training these young men and women to remain peaceful when faced with hatred and violence at the hands of police as well as angry white counter-demonstrators. You feel responsible for the students; for many, it's the first time they've ever faced an out-of-control mob. Things are heating up—people are yelling, making threats, and pushing the students. You place yourself in between the students and their assailants.

Suddenly, a burly slab of a white man accosts you, scream-ing racial epithets; without warning, he rears back and spits in your face. His face is a mask of hatred—defying you to strike back. You want to. Your rage—and the collective rage of centuries of oppression—is rising inside, threatening to spill out. But you've trained for this moment. You look the man in the eyes, searching for something you can connect to. He looks like a biker. Holding his gaze, you ask if he's got a motorcycle or a hot rod. This is not the response he expected. Taken aback, he mumbles that he has a motorcycle. You say, "Yeah, me too. I love mine. By the way, do you have a handkerchief?" Before he realizes what he's doing, he pulls one out and hands it over. You wipe off the spit and start asking about technical details—comparing how your bikes are customized, their horsepower, engine capacity, and so on. Gradually, the hatred leaves his face, replaced with the joy of someone who shares your passion for the open road. Because you've acknowledged his humanity, he's starting to see yours. After a while, this man who seemed bent on destroying you asks if there's any way he can help you in the work you're doing.

This is a true event. It happened to Rev. James Lawson, a civil rights leader. I've taken some liberties in my description, but one thing is certain: most of us, in his shoes, would have lashed out; we would not have been able to transform hatred into harmony. What the story demonstrates is that it's possible: there is a force inside you that can transform the worst part of you into the best. Not only that, it has the power to inspire the same alchemy in those around you. This is the breathtaking power of Goodness.

WHY IS IT SO HARD TO BE GOOD?

Most people genuinely yearn to be good, to do the "right" thing. If you've made the effort to read this book and use the tools, you're clearly trying to become a better version of yourself. So why do you so often feel like you're failing?

It's because Part X has defined goodness in a way that guarantees failure. Deep down, it has convinced us that the way to be "good" is to eliminate all traces of "badness" inside. That's impossible, but we buy into it because we desperately want to see ourselves as good—we'll even deny the bad things we do in order to maintain that image of ourselves.

Underneath the surface of every human being there lurks a dark force that destroys any chance of our being wholly "good." That force has always been described as *evil*. It's in all of us—and it doesn't go away. If you think it's possible for a person to eliminate all traces of evil inside, just look around you: Do you know anyone who has attained a state of pure goodness—not most of the time, not some of the time, but all the time? With no indulgences, no outbursts, no hidden feelings of superiority or inferiority? No critical judgments of others? I've never met anyone who lives consistently in this elevated state. If a human being were that pure, they wouldn't be human. In fact, to be fully human is to feel these two opposites—good and evil, light and dark—coexisting inside you.

THE DENIAL OF EVIL BEGETS EVIL

Why would Part X want to convince you that you can eradicate all traces of evil within you? Because if you keep trying and failing, eventually you'll tell yourself you've succeeded even though you haven't: "I've gotten rid of the evil inside me. *I am pure.*"

There are examples everywhere. Each week, we see public figures who present themselves as beyond reproach and then get caught with their hands in the cookie jar; a journalist hypes his objectivity while making up false news stories; a Bible-thumping preacher exalts the sanctity of marriage while having an affair; a financial advisor insists his clients' welfare comes first while he steers them to investments that pay him the highest commissions. It's easy to condemn these people as con artists, but the self-aggrandizement isn't just to fool their audiences—*it's to fool themselves!* It's a way of convincing themselves, "I've done it ... I've rid myself of evil." Rather than admitting they have evil inside them—and will have to fight it for the rest of their lives—they have let Part X convince them their work is done.

You don't have to be in the public eye nor do your actions have to be criminal or extreme for you to declare yourself free of evil. We all do it at one point or another, thinking we're above reproach. But when you position yourself as all good, you become superior to anyone who disagrees with you; suddenly *they're* the only ones who need to work on themselves. Here's an example everyone's experienced: You're sitting around the dinner table with your family, and a political argument starts. You believe strongly that any good person would have to see things your way. To your surprise, there are family members who don't agree. As emotions rise, a kind of self-righteousness takes over. You wonder how these ignorant people could be in the same family as you. Whether you realize it or not, you've begun to hate them; they've become the enemy. Deep down, you've positioned yourself as all good. Whoever disagrees with you, you regard as evil, which makes them worthy targets of your unrestrained wrath. The next day, you wake up feeling sheepish, as if you were temporarily insane the night before—subject to a blind passion that consumed all balance and restraint. If you're honest with yourself, you'll recognize that you've vilified and hurt people you love, speaking to them in ways you'd never want to be spoken to. *By denying your own capacity for evil, you became evil.*

It's understandable that you want to see yourself as good; goodness is the deepest, most profound spiritual experience you can have. The problem occurs when Part X convinces you you're *all* good—without any evil inside. Once it succeeds, you become the vehicle for the worst kind of evil. If Reverend Lawson had fallen prey to Part X, he *wouldn't* have restrained himself. He and his white adversary would have become mirror images—each bringing out the worst in the other. If you examine any intractable conflict—ethnic, religious, or interpersonal—you'll see this cycle of mutual dehumanization. Each side sees itself as pure good and the other as pure evil.

So if Goodness isn't the elimination of evil, what is it?

GOOD *VERSUS* GOODNESS

Notice I used the term *Goodness*, not the word *Good*. From here on, it's important to distinguish between the two. This isn't some nitpicking affectation, it's a crucial step in dealing with evil, because "good" and "goodness" are actually *opposites*. That's right, they're opposites.

"Good" is an illusory state in which you believe all evil has been cleansed from your psyche. If you persist in this delusion, there's no need to monitor how you treat other people. Having rid yourself of evil, you can do no wrong. A grotesque example of this delusional superiority is the doctrine of racial purity promulgated in the early twentieth century by Adolf Hitler. In Hitler's deranged psyche, if you weren't pure Aryan, you were evil and subject for extermination. When he imprisoned and killed Jews, Slavs, Gypsies, and other "impure" groups, he believed he was acting on behalf of good—keeping the Germanic identity unspoiled by inferior genetic and racial strains.

If you're telling yourself "I'm not Hitler," you're right, but you've missed the point. All of us want to see ourselves as good, and find ways to become part of a superior group, free of the failings we see in others. Every in-group—the financial elite of society, a street gang, the "mean girls" in high school, etc.—is influenced by this lie; even religions can declare themselves "superior." The essence of an in-group is that it claims to be pure and good, while the rest of the world is evil.

You don't even have to be part of an *actual* in-group to wear the mantle of superiority. Everyone, at one point or another, becomes an "in-group of one" in the privacy of their own mind. This usually takes the form of habits you'd never think of as evil. Be honest with yourself about how you treat the people around you. Have you ever ignored someone in need because you were in a hurry or had "more important things" to do? Have you ever left a mess someplace where someone else would have to clean it up? How about getting back at someone because of something they did to you?

You're barely aware of these habits; it wouldn't occur to you that they are small, everyday acts of evil—and yet they are. And you wouldn't be able to rationalize them unless, deep inside, you'd convinced yourself that you're better and more deserving than the people around you. In a sense, this everyday evil does even more harm than the dramatic, public displays we've cited. There are so many instances of these more commonplace acts, and we're so inured to them that they slip by our defenses unnoticed. They infect us like an invisible virus, dominating our habits and weakening our moral instincts. And this goes on in every human being every single day.

The truth is, humanity has been duped by Part X. It paints being "good" as the state of ultimate advancement, when really it's a giant step backwards. No matter what rules you follow, books you read, or rituals you perform, that "damned spot" of evil can't be removed. So here we are, wanting to feel good about ourselves, yet knowing we have a built-in store of evil that can't be eradicated. How do we solve the conundrum?

The answer involves a small change in terminology and a huge change in orientation. Terminology first: Your goal needs to change from being "good" to maintaining a state of "Goodness." "Good," as should now be clear, is a fiction, a permanent state of purity that no one can attain. "Good" is what you claim to be. "Goodness" is what you do right now, in the present. It isn't a black belt in morality; it's an ongoing process that requires your ongoing participation.

How can you participate? First, forget about reaching a final victory that eliminates all evil. That's the lie Part X sold you. Your new orientation isn't centered on vanquishing evil—its focus is on the endless process of transmuting evil into something positive. We'd like to imagine we can make evil disappear in one, decisive victory. But evil won't cooperate; it reappears endlessly. You attain Goodness by transforming it every time it returns. That's what Goodness is: *the ceaseless commitment to transform evil.*

TRANSFORMING EVIL

For most people, the word *transformation* brings up images of a caterpillar becoming a butterfly. That image applies to life-forms that lack free will (the caterpillar doesn't *choose* to become a butterfly; it happens automatically). But human beings are given a choice whether or not to evolve. Evil *forces* us to choose: either we give in to it, or we use it to become better versions of ourselves.

Truth, Beauty, and Goodness all have a unique contribution to this transformational process. Truth *reveals* Part X—enabling us to see how it convinces us of our purity. Beauty *inspires* us to fight X, to strive for greater honesty. And Goodness *transforms* us—allowing us to leverage evil into virtue.

You've already seen examples of this leveraging process in prior chapters. Marty used the Black Sun every time he wanted to lose his temper—he became a leader in his family. Beth used the Vortex every time she was tempted to withdraw from her daughter and customers—she learned to give more of herself. In each case, by recognizing their own version of inner evil, and using the tools again and again, they became better people—with a more positive impact on the people around them. That's what we mean by transforming evil.

The traditional model required you to eradicate evil permanently. In the new model, you face it every day and use tools that transform it into Goodness. As strange as it sounds, good and evil become partners in creating a new you—more virtuous than you ever imagined you could be. Evil is no longer the obstacle to evolution; it becomes the force that propels it.

As in the case of Truth and Beauty, there are three principles that will enable you to know whether you're transforming evil into Goodness or falling prey to Part X's false version—purity.

PRINCIPLE 1: GOODNESS REQUIRES INSTINCTS, NOT EDICTS

You've learned you have evil inside you, and your job is to transform it every time it comes up. But to transform evil, you need something *stronger* than evil. Since evil is a force, you need a counterforce. Traditionally, that's not the way we go about fighting evil. We think we can ensure

against evil by adhering to a set of rules that govern our behavior. The rules may be codified in laws or ethical principles; they may have ancient roots or derive from modern
tradition; they may be given to us by our religion, parents,
or culture. But they all have something in common: they're
just words. They proscribe evil, but don't give us the power
to transform it.

Words are ineffective for many reasons. First, evil is
alive—it's a force attacking you from within all the time. In
Chapter 3, when Marty was exploding with rage every time
his son wanted to play a videogame, would an edict—"Never
lose your temper"—have stopped him? No. Words can *guide*
you, but they don't have the power to fight Part X when it
floods you.

Moreover, words are subject to interpretation. Look no
further than the unspeakable violence historically committed
in the name of holy scripture and you'll realize that words not
only lack the power to stop evil, they can easily be twisted to
justify it. The truth is, only tools, and the life energy released
by them, have the power to transform the evil buried inside us.

Life moves quickly and we must make moral decisions in
the midst of ever-shifting circumstances. No fixed set of laws
or ethical injunctions can hope to cover all the possibilities
generated by this powerful, moving reality. "Thou shalt not
kill" is something we can all agree on, but what if you have
the chance to kill a crazed gunman and save a classroom of
kids he's taken hostage? You don't have time to think, let
alone consult with a lawyer or religious scholar—you have to
act. And to get yourself to act morally, you need something

that moves with the same speed as the infinitely changing circumstances you find yourself in: you need a force.

Fortunately, we have the force of Goodness inside us. It consists of our moral instincts. These instincts can be honed and developed in the battle with your own evil. But how can you be sure you're right about what is evil inside you? Should you study the great philosophers? Is the secret to notice what makes you feel guilty? Is the evil part of you the part your parents were most critical of?

None of the above. Evil doesn't reveal itself to your intellect. You don't need a logical explanation for why something is evil. As we've said, in any given situation it's your *instincts* that can sense what's evil. A perfect example of this was voiced by Supreme Court Justice Potter Stewart. The court was deciding a case that hinged on whether a film was pornographic. Stewart was unable to define in words what pornography was, but said, "I know it when I see it." His words are among the most frequently quoted from any Supreme Court decision. His point is well taken. There are things that can't be defined in words; they must be recognized by gut instinct.

To find your inner evil, start with what you've been reading about since Chapter 1: Part X. By now you should be clear on how it sabotages you—getting you to give in to destructive impulses, flooding you with worries, convincing you to procrastinate, etc. Normally, you wouldn't think of these self-defeating behaviors as "evil." But consider their impact on the people around you. If you're overweight and Part X keeps seducing you off your diet, you may be creating anxiety for your family and burdening them with future medical expenses. If you worry chronically, you may be depressing to be around. If you procrastinate, you're probably letting other people down—or forcing them to do the things you're avoiding. The moment you consider the impact your Part X has on the people around you, it becomes easy to identify it as evil.

Beyond Part X, examine your everyday habits, at home, work, and in social settings, especially the habits that damage your relationships to the people around you. Look for small acts of rudeness, disinterest, selfishness, cheating, and so on. Every single person who has ever lived—no matter how saintly—is guilty of these lapses. Whether you attribute these habits to Part X or not, train yourself to recognize and label them as evil right in the moment.

Finally, try to correct these habits; at the very least, admit them and apologize for their impact on others. As you do—if you pay careful attention—you'll feel the force of Goodness beginning to move through you. It's a giving force. Considerate of the people around you, Goodness *wants* to do the right thing in each moment, and it doesn't care whether these unselfish acts are rewarded or not. Unhurried and silent, this force will turn its healing powers on even the smallest expression of evil. It's the bearer of love throughout the universe.

PRINCIPLE 2: GOODNESS HURTS

Goodness requires that you monitor your bad habits, identify the damage you inflict on those around you, admit it openly, change those habits . . . and keep doing it for the rest of your life. Goodness is hard, ongoing work, which makes it painful.

Goodness also hurts because it's humbling. Deep down, we all want to *deny* inner evil. We have no problem seeing it in others, but we like to think of ourselves as all good. It's humbling to admit you have evil in you, but without embracing that pain, you can't flow with Goodness. A film called *The Apostle* depicts this kind of pain beautifully. Robert Duvall plays a charismatic preacher struggling to face his version of evil (he's killed his wife's lover in fit of rage). He also has to overcome evil in the form of a racist construction worker who threatens to bulldoze Duvall's multiracial church. In an emotional scene, Duvall, seeing goodness in the man, approaches him with love and understanding, and the man admits he doesn't really want to knock the church down. Duvall says, "I know. That's why I'll kneel with you, pray with you, cry with you, do anything . . . because I know you're a good man." The man starts to cry. He admits, "I'm embarrassed." Duvall tells him he understands: "I was a worse sinner than you in my time. Go ahead, brother, cry . . . I'll cry with you."

It's painful to bare the worst parts of your soul. But if you're serious about channeling Goodness, this pain can't remain abstract; you'll have to experience it for yourself. This exercise will give you a taste of it:

- Think about a bad habit of yours that mars your relationship with the world or hurts the people around you. Maybe you lose your temper and become disrespectful. Maybe you withdraw from people when they need you the most—they feel abandoned. Maybe you're inattentive and disorganized, and other people have to clean up after you.
- Whatever habit you choose, close your eyes and admit it: "This habit is evil; it hurts people, damages my relationships, and diminishes me as a human being. There is no excuse for it." Take note of how that admission feels.
- Now imagine admitting that truth every time you lapse into the habit. How does that feel?

We rarely allow ourselves to feel humbled like this, because we're pain-avoidant. That's what makes the false version of goodness so tempting. You get to think of yourself as all good, denying the evil that's alive and well inside you.

PRINCIPLE 3: GOODNESS REQUIRES ONGOING ACTION

Once you can strip down and admit you have evil inside you, you have to take contrary action—do exactly the opposite of what evil is telling you to do. If you habitually lose your temper, you'll have to control yourself. If you withdraw from people, you'll have to give more of yourself. If you over-rely on others, you'll have to do more for yourself.

But taking action means more than just correcting your

bad habits in the outside world. There's also *inner* action. Using a tool, labeling Part X, and even restraining your impulses are inner actions. They're "actions" because they require effort and their goal is to make a change in your inner world. The combination of these inner and outer actions make Goodness more than just an abstract idea; it becomes a way of life. Here's how to put this into practice:

- Go back to the bad habit you identified in the last exercise. Think of some corrective actions you could take. One might be to admit to someone that you're aware of the habit and the harm it does; another might be to use a tool to help you refrain from it the next time it comes up; another might be to make amends to the people who've been hurt by it. Whatever action you choose—whether it's inner or outer—muster up the determination to do it.
- Now imagine taking that action (and others as they occur to you) as the weeks, months, and years stretch into the future—every time you feel yourself falling prey to the bad habit. Each time you do this, you're transforming evil, creating Goodness over a long period of time. See if you get an intuition about what kind of person you become as you maintain this practice. What does it feel like to be this new "you"?

Part X will try to convince you it's impossible to become this person. That's a lie. All it requires is ongoing effort. And the payoff is worth it. Each time you follow your instincts and do the right thing, you'll feel another drop of Goodness flowing into your life. You'll be surprised at how meaning-ful life becomes when you dedicate it to something higher than yourself. You'll also be surprised at how the people around you respond. When you transform inner evil into Goodness, you inspire those around you to do the same. They might not know you're working on yourself, but they'll be drawn to your Goodness. When you shine brightly, others yearn to as well. Reverend Lawson was a good example: by taking the high road, he gave his attacker the opportunity to become a better man. His life became a conduit through which Goodness transformed the world.

ASCENDING TO A HIGHER WORLD

Part X never gives up, but as strange as it sounds, that's good news. It means that every single day is filled with op-portunities to fight. Whether you win or lose any one battle, your Life Force will increase. You'll see the immediate re-sults: more energy and enthusiasm, increased productivity, decreased stress, and, most important, a growing sense of possibility: if you can dream it and act upon it, anything can happen.

But that's only the beginning. Over time, the Life Force will send three emissaries—Truth, Beauty, and Goodness—to help you continue your ascent. Like hidden allies you never knew existed, these representatives of the Life Force want to help you climb the path to your highest potential.

Truth will keep you honest—it will *reveal* the ongoing

ways Part X lies to you. Beauty will *inspire* you to fight those lies and live with integrity. And Goodness will *transform* you—giving you the power to change evil into virtue. With these three guides along your path, you cannot fail to ascend to a whole new world.

Chapter Eight

The New World

Phil describes the Higher and Lower Worlds and explains how we humans are in a unique position to reconnect these worlds by doing the inner work to heal ourselves.

Barry just described three ways the Higher World begins to appear to someone as their Life Force develops. Truth, Beauty, and Goodness are emissaries of that Higher World, pieces of it that reach down into the Lower World we inhabit. Like the first few swollen drops of summer rain that fall on your head, waking you up to the immense power of the thunderclouds above, Truth, Beauty, and Goodness "reach down" from the Higher World above us so we can experience them in our world.

There's more to the Higher World than Truth, Beauty, and Goodness, but most of it can't reach down to connect to us; we have to reach up to it. When you do, you'll discover not just new experiences, but an entire world waiting for you.

Most people don't know how to reach up and connect to this new world. They live and die without ever experiencing what lies beyond the world of our five senses. Without being able to experience this Higher World, you'll go through life without peace, faith, or a real sense of meaning. The tools can remedy this, but you'll need to see their power in a new light and, most important, use them with a different purpose. Most people use the tools to address a particular problem, and when the problem is solved they forget about the tool. They've used the tool to climb out of whatever hole they're in, they experience the relief of being free from what's been bothering them, and then they go on with their life.

They're missing something. Abandoning the use of tools once your problem is solved is like leaving the theater before the final act. The tools don't just help you climb out of a particular hole. They can take you far beyond relief from specific symptoms like exhaustion, depression, craving, and so on. If you keep using them, you ascend to another state—another world, filled with limitless potential.

But most people just want to get by. They lack the imagination and willpower to go beyond solving their immediate problems. It's impossible to talk someone into believing the Higher World—with its limitless possibilities—is real. They'll need to experience it for themselves. But that's not so easy.

When you look around you, are you inspired by what you see? For most of us, the answer is no. Your job bores you, your kids won't behave, and the incessant traffic makes you late. Your energy is drained by mechanical tasks, petty disputes, and endless responsibilities. And if you look beyond your personal life, the picture darkens even further: political chaos, earthquakes, mega-storms, poverty, starvation, and violence on our streets and beyond our borders—the problems unfurl without end.

Nothing in that description feels "Higher." In fact, it's an apt description of a "Lower World," a kind of hell. Not the kind of hell organized religion imagines as a place you enter after your physical death; rather, it's a here-and-now kind of hell, a "hell on earth." Which brings up the question: why is it so easy to see the Lower World all around us, yet so difficult to see the Higher World or even to believe it's real?

The answer is simple: Part X *blinds* you to the Higher World. Every time it creates a problem you don't know how to solve, you wind up in a hole. From there, all you can see is the hole you're in; you can't see beyond it. *What we believe to be real is limited to what we perceive with our senses.* Our ancestors were unable to "see" anything beyond a flat world; they couldn't believe they could sail west without dropping off the edge of the earth. That's a real limitation.

The modern human being faces a different kind of limitation. In Columbus's time, what people couldn't "see" was a huge part of their own world; what we can't perceive now is *another world.* But in both cases, the assumption is that if something can't be perceived, it doesn't exist. *That's* why we're blind to the Higher World.

This leads to a Part X trap. If you can't perceive anything outside the "hole" X has thrown you into, you'll have no incentive to find that Higher World. In case a bit of hope or a sense of possibility breaks through, Part X will attack them as wishful thinking. It tells you, "If the Higher World really existed, it would be obvious; the troubled mess you see around you is all there is. Stop searching for something that doesn't exist."

Part X is lulling you to sleep. It's a dangerous sleep, the equivalent of a nap in your car with the motor running and the windows sealed. You may not smell the carbon monoxide as you nod off, but that doesn't mean it won't kill you. It's a subtle kind of death, an appeal to the laziness that afflicts most of us. It would be disastrous if there were no Higher World: life would have no meaning; death would be intolerable. But that's not the problem.

The Higher World is real, but unlike the Lower World we see around us every day, it can't be experienced with our five senses. X says that means it doesn't exist—another lie. You can absolutely experience a Higher World and reap the benefits of its infinite power. But our five senses—seeing, hearing, tasting, smelling, and feeling—can't perceive that world. You need a "sixth sense," and unlike the five we're born with, you have to intentionally develop your sixth sense.

This sixth sense is the Life Force itself. As we use the tools to work through problems in our lives, we build our Life Force. But once we've solved a problem a few times—and it no longer seems like such a threat—we have a tendency to stop using the tools. This is a form of spiritual arrogance. As strange as it may sound, we tell ourselves that because we *know* how to repel a symptom (let's say using the Mother tool to counteract demoralization), we don't have to actually *use the tool* any longer. Sounds crazy, but from Part X's point of view it makes sense.

X is the sworn enemy of your Life Force. It wants you to

use the tools as little as possible, because using them makes your Life Force stronger. It whispers in your ear that you don't have to use the tools as long as you understand how they work. But if you want to build stronger muscles, you can't just think about lifting weights—you actually have to do the exercises.

In the same way, if you want to increase your Life Force, you have to actually use the tools. This turns the meaning of problems upside down. Rather than seeing them as obstacles, you realize that they are motivators, reminders to use a tool. In this context, it becomes clear the tools can do more than relieve symptoms: they can give you the ability to see the Higher World.

We call this the "higher use of tools." Using the tools this way can seem counterintuitive at first. Here's how the process works:

- Problems keep coming, requiring you to keep using the tools.
- The more you use the tools, the stronger your Life Force grows.
- The Life Force is the source of your sixth sense.
- As your sixth sense develops, you can perceive the Higher World.

With the above sequence in mind, every problem becomes a gift. Just the way a good martial artist will use their opponent's own force against them, you're taking the problems X creates and using them to stimulate your own Life Force. This turns the tables on Part X. The worse the problem it creates, the deeper it throws you into the hole, the more Life Force you develop. The tools work like a spiritual slingshot, using the very things X uses to trap you in the Lower World to propel you into the Higher World.

But Part X never gives up. It will keep on sending you problems, some new, some old. You can choose to see these problems as bad luck or unwarranted punishment and let them paralyze you—which is exactly the way Part X hopes you react—or you can choose to see each problem as a signal to use a tool.

The four tools in this book weren't selected at random. You may have already noticed that each of them moves your energy upward. In the Vortex and the Tower, your entire body moves upward; in the Black Sun and the Mother, a part of you moves upward. What's the significance of this upward movement?

Each tool, in its own way, involves an "ascension" to a Higher World. But this upward journey isn't a metaphor picked arbitrarily to symbolize spiritual growth. It's a real journey involving real forces. And the first part of the journey isn't up, it's down. You fall into a hole and you use the tools to "ascend" out of it.

To reap the benefits of the higher use of tools, you have to *actively* accept these cycles. That means when Part X throws you down into the "hole" (of deprivation, depletion, demoralization, victimization), rather than just tolerating the discomfort, you need to enter into the pain more deeply. The more you feel the pain, the more you'll be able to transform it.

The ancient Greeks (and many other cultures) saw this

idea reflected in the cycles of death and rebirth, especially in nature. Winter inevitably comes, but we can have faith it's always followed by spring. In the same way, you can have faith that the Life Force, newly strengthened, will bring you back "up" again. The details change from person to person, but the underlying meaning is that when you face death, your courage is rewarded with a vision of the Higher World.

This new awareness is quite different from the clarity of eyesight. Seeing something with your eyes puts a distance between you and it. "Seeing" the Higher World has more of the quality of going "inside" something, becoming one with it. Only your sixth sense can accomplish this.

Being able to perceive the Higher World creates the sense that something completely different from what we're used to in everyday life exists. And whatever this indefinable thing is, it radiates peace, harmony, and love for all beings. Not because a god-figure orders it, but because these energies flow naturally from the Higher World as it seeks what *it* needs: the interconnection of all life in the universe.

The Higher World overcomes the sense of impossibility Part X inflicts on you, because the Higher World is *made of possibility*. Nothing is more inspiring than witnessing the Higher World do what seems impossible—whether in a single human life, in society at large, or in the rejuvenation of the entire earth. This victory of the possible over the impossible, of life over death, of yes over no, creates a joy you'll never forget.

THE ATTACK ON WONDER

There's a final obstacle to overcome in your journey to the Higher World. It's your skepticism. This shouldn't be a surprise—Western culture has spent the last two millennia making it increasingly difficult for us to believe in a Higher World. It wasn't always this way. More than two thousand years ago, Plato, the father of Western philosophy, saw the spiritual world as the only true reality. What we now consider the "real" and only world, he saw as an illusion.

He presented this in his famous allegory of the cave. Imagine someone who spent his entire life in a cave, chained to the wall, unable to even turn his head, forced to stare at a blank wall. Behind him (and out of his view) is a fire. Real people and objects pass in front of the fire and project shadows on the wall. True reality is behind him, but all he sees are the phantom images projected in front of him. *He is forced to believe the images are reality.*

Plato felt the role of philosophy was to free mankind to perceive reality in its true form. But how do you see the light of reality when you don't even know it exists? Plato's answer was that there's a specific state of mind that gives you the vision you need to penetrate the unknown. That state of mind is called *wonder.*

Imagine yourself encountering an invisible world incomprehensibly bigger and wiser than you are: a mysterious, ungraspable world, full of meaning and promise, peeking through the surface of the "real world." You'd be overcome with awe and wonder. If you weren't amazed, it would mean you'd lost touch with this Higher World and its miraculous aliveness. This was what led Plato to his famous maxim "Philosophy begins with wonder."

Plato's student Aristotle reinterpreted Plato's idea and defined *wonder* in a much more limited way, reducing it to the uncomfortable puzzlement you feel when you don't understand something. Aristotle wanted us to use our thinking minds to eliminate ignorance. Plato wanted us to live in awe. The beauty of the Higher World was gradually lost because we began to view its mysteries as if they were simple problems to be solved.

Losing our sense of wonder took a tremendous toll on the human race. It shut the door to the Higher World, forcing us to get what we needed from the earth. This had a good side: it demanded that we become more independent, culminating in the development of science and a much deeper understanding of the physical world surrounding us.

But we live in an age where science insists there is no Higher World. If that were true, there would be nothing to be in awe of. We need awe to remind us there is something bigger and wiser than we are. Without it, our egos—convinced they know everything—feel free to make their own rules. Greed, selfishness, and lack of responsibility for anyone but ourselves have taken over our culture, deforming and weakening it. Most dangerous of all, the combined power of science and industry has far outstripped our ability to hold these lower forces at bay. Like biblical punishments visited upon the earth, terrorism, ethnic warfare, and environmental destruction run rampant.

This loss of our sense of wonder couldn't have happened without Part X working behind the scenes. As it gained more and more influence over each individual, it was also advancing its collective goals for society—goals that can only be described as evil. The attack on wonder is a crucial part of its strategy, because as it destroys our ability to connect with the Higher World, we lose the ability to fight back or even to understand what we're fighting against.

Historically, our opponent in this cosmic battle has been called the Devil, and the force it commands, the force we must defeat, is called evil. We live in a time of individuality. That means each of us is out there on our own, so to speak, vulnerable to attack by evil. And the soldier of evil, its representative in this inner war, is Part X.

Even though X attacks through the medium of psychological problems, and even though those problems differ from person to person, its overarching goal is the same in every situation: to block the evolution of the entire human race. Because Part X works on this collective level, subjecting all of us to its evil designs, it deserves the title of Devil.

Over thousands of years, every religion has had its own version of the Devil—a being that works ceaselessly to "collect" human souls. But what does this mean? Collecting a soul isn't a physical act like collecting apples in a basket. It's an inner process, designed to destroy our sense of wonder and replace it with the worship of our own ego. "I'm amazed" is replaced with "I know."

But how is that collecting a soul? It's not like what you see in books and movies where the Devil openly offers to trade some glittery prize in exchange for the immortal part of a person. The modern, twenty-first-century Devil has a much more sophisticated way to collect souls. He doesn't collect them one at a time; he gets them wholesale. And he doesn't catch them in a net or a pail; *he uses an entire world.*

In all cultures, the Lower World is ruled by the Devil. Every person trapped in this Lower World—their sense of wonder taken from them by a skeptical culture—has been "caught" by the Devil. The Devil needs no walls or cages to keep you under his power. If he can keep you from believing there is a Higher World, then you'll look for all your needs to be satisfied in the Lower World. All he has to do is sit back and watch as you get caught deeper and deeper in the Lower World.

THE FALL OF A WORLD

If you were to ask yourself what is meant by "the fall of man," you probably think of the story of Adam and Eve in the Old Testament. This was basically a story about human beings lapsing into sin. But Adam and Eve's actions didn't only affect man, they affected the whole world. Sin, brought into the world by their actions, contaminated the world that God had created. It broke off part of the Higher World, and Adam and Eve "fell" into this new Lower World of death, illness, injustice, and evil.

And once death became an issue for people, so did survival. The Lower World couldn't create new life the way the Higher World could—it was a place of scarcity. In this limited world, we turned against one another because we perceived there wasn't enough to go around. The best we could do was to fend off our individual deaths as long as possible. Life became a vicious game of musical chairs—each time the music stopped, someone had to die.

The Higher World isn't indifferent to the suffering of human beings trapped in this cosmic slum. It has more than enough life to give to the Lower World, but *it has no way to get that energy into that world*. It's like the moving van arrives with everything you need to furnish a new house, but there's no key. Something needs to act as a connector between the Higher World and the Lower World—a spiritual key.

Only one thing in the universe was suitable to make that connection. It had to be something capable of entering *both worlds*. Only a human being could do that. It's part of the great paradox of being human: we can be part of the lowest and the highest *at the same time*.

But mankind has a motivational problem. We have no trouble working on our own potential. The motivation is obvious—we want power, fame, brilliance, etc.—things that make us "great." But very often our desire for these personal rewards pushes aside something more important. If we want to be the connector between the Higher and Lower Worlds, we have to go beyond our individual needs.

RECONNECTING THE TWO WORLDS

Let's say you've taken an afternoon off from work to finish reading this book. One of the chapters applies directly to you; you want to read it again and practice the tool it describes. Just at that moment, a neighbor knocks on your door. His car battery is dead—he calls out your name and asks if you're home and could you help him get a jump.

It's the middle of the day. There's no reason for him to expect you'd be there. You stay perfectly quiet and in a few minutes he walks away, never suspecting you were hiding. Now you have a few undisturbed hours to really zero in on the chapter. As you bring your focus back to the book, you feel a twinge of guilt. But you override it, telling yourself your personal evolution is more important than his car problem. You congratulate yourself on your dedication to the book.

Are you correct about your decision? Did you just take a step in your own evolution? The answer is no. By not putting the book aside for a few minutes and helping your neighbor, you *delayed* your evolution. At the moment you turned back to the book, you gave in to Part X—even though you were reading about *how to defeat Part X*.

You may object, "The book is about how to find the Higher World . . . isn't that what I just did?" No, you're confusing the ideas in the book with the inner state you're in. The subject matter might be spiritual, but your state of mind was self-absorbed—the "What's in it for me?" attitude. Self-absorption is a state of constant contraction, but the Higher World is constantly expanding. Contracting energy can't connect to an expanding world.

Our culture deals with this problem by denial. By telling us we live in a dead universe, a place with no conscious awareness, it also tells us that we needn't worry about our inner state—there's no one there to care.

But the Higher World isn't limited the way the Lower World is. It's alive and aware even if it's not apparent to us. We're accustomed to think of consciousness and its sibling— meaning—as things that happen inside our skulls; the notion that we could experience them as flowing unrestricted through the cosmos sounds like a fairy tale.

Which is why many challenge the idea that the universe is alive and aware. Their objection, which is understandable, is that they've never experienced this alive cosmos; they've neither seen nor felt it.

It's true they've felt very little of the creativity, freedom, and abundance that we've defined as their cosmic birthright. Their experience of life has been competitive, painful, demanding—followed by death. But that doesn't refute the existence of the expansive cosmos we've talked about. All it reveals is that it takes a great deal more work to see the Higher World than it does to see the Lower World.

That's why you need to maintain a state of spiritual generosity: a state of constant giving, motivated by the faith that when life seems to interfere with your personal journey, it's really guiding you to the set of actions that will allow that journey to continue. It's not a path you can find through thinking; it's a path that only becomes visible when you *surrender to what life demands of you.*

Let's return to your secret study session in your home. Your neighbor—only half expecting you to be home—quickly gave up. You greedily take advantage of the extra hours, reading the chapter that interests you several times and practicing the tool. When it's over, to your surprise and disappointment, you're not overflowing with life. You're exhausted. You take a nap.

You wake up unrefreshed—and vaguely guilty. Not because of your neighbor's plight—he got a jump from someone else. Your guilt is because you've failed to help the Higher World redeem its fallen Lower part.

But life gives you another chance. You look out your window and see your neighbor has returned. The look on his face tells you something is bothering him. Fearing he's discovered your ruse that afternoon, you go outside to apologize. But he's not thinking about that at all. He wants your advice about his teenage son who's fallen into a withdrawn, demoralized state.

The chapter you were reading was about exactly that problem. You invite him into your house and hand him the book. The copy is dog-eared and marked up; he says it looks like you're still reading it yourself. A voice in your head tells you not to give him the book; you're not finished with it. But some higher generosity takes over. You hand him the book and tell him you can discuss it tomorrow.

Unlike the exhaustion and guilt you felt after "studying" the book for your own advancement, the simple act of *giving the book away* leaves you with a vital feeling of life and its possibilities. You feel like the world is on your side.

This story reveals the secret of healing: in giving the book away, you acknowledged there were things in life more important than your personal goals—and that you were willing to put those goals on hold if a higher demand was placed on you.

The Life Force you're seeking is only granted when you behave—*behave*, not read, memorize, or explain—in an expansive way. Here, that meant giving away the book to help someone else rather than reading it to help yourself. Taking this generous action was an expression of faith in the Higher World. If that world does indeed contain infinite forces, it doesn't matter how many books you give away—there will always be more.

A NEW SET OF PRIORITIES

The task of redeeming the Lower World transcends everything else in importance. This creates a paradox. Only by accepting that the fate of the world is more important than pursuing your own desires will you yourself be healed and have enough life energy to pursue your own personal goals.

When you avoided your neighbor in need so you could study the book for your own benefit, you ended up depleted. The words you were reading described expansiveness, but your actions were selfish, so your energy contracted. It was only when you gave the book away that you reached a state of expansiveness allowing you to connect to the Higher World. When life presents you with someone in need, rather than see them as a threat, see them as an opportunity to put yourself in this expansive state. It's only when you give without expecting anything in return that you become fully alive.

Because everything depends on recognizing these opportunities to expand—and because our instincts make us self-absorbed and contracted—you don't want to miss an opportunity to activate your Higher Self. Here are three of the biggest ways you can do that:

- Giving to someone when you have nothing to gain for yourself
- Performing generous acts that no one is aware of (even the recipient)
- Helping someone else at a personal cost (for example, canceling your vacation in order to stay with a close friend who is ill)

HIGHER SELF *VERSUS* LOWER SELF

We live in a self-absorbed, competitive culture: getting left behind by others is terrifying and failing is unacceptable. The pressure this creates keeps us in a state of perpetual contraction, unable to be fully alive. The solution I'm offering may seem radical, even foolish: encouraging you to give things away (not just material things but control, status, adoration, etc.) to serve a Higher World that you can't see.

When presented with this new way of living, most of us are skeptical. We've spent most of our lives pursuing what we think of as personal success, focused on what we want for ourselves. This gives us our identity. The idea that life will change for the better when we become less self-absorbed feels like a sucker's bet.

The irony is that I'm not asking you to lose your identity; I'm asking you to find it. Finding yourself is a paradox. You become your real, Higher Self by putting your personal goals second and the Higher World's first. Only in this role of helping and service do you expand into full aliveness. And only in this fully alive state can you be a bridge between the Higher and Lower Worlds.

Your "reward" for being a conduit will be enough life energy to pursue your own goals. Notice I didn't say "identify" your own goals, I said "pursue" them. Your Higher Self isn't activated by theories or discussions. It comes alive when you are *taking action* that moves you toward your goal. Identity isn't an idea; it's the way you act in the world.

If we understand identity this way, most people have little contact with their real, or Higher, Self. The actions they take are little more than mindless habits. They feel familiar due to repetition, but they lack free will or creativity. Some obvious examples include hours spent in front of the TV, computer, or phone; rewarding yourself with drugs, food, and alcohol after work; taking your frustrations out on your spouse because he or she is right there.

These behaviors appeal to our ego, or Lower Self, not to our real self. The ego is the king of the superficial. Everything it has or wants comes from the world outside it. All it cares about is what it can get for itself from that world.

Because it's superficial, it borrows an identity from those around it. It says you are where you live, who your friends are, what you listen to, etc. If this sounds like high school, it is—but it's a high school most of us have never graduated from. You're still playing at the shallow end of the pool, lacking the tools, the courage, and the faith to make your own way through life.

That's why it's not so easy to get someone to step out from behind their ego hiding place. We hold on to our egos for dear life because we believe (mistakenly) that what our egos want is what we really need. The ego wants three things: the approval, validation, and adoration of others; immediate gratification of its physical needs and desires; and to be "right."

These selfish demands paint an ugly picture of our Lower Self. Still, it's not so easy to convince someone to slip out of their self-absorbed skin. One reason is because it only looks ugly when you see it in others. When it overtakes you, these behaviors seem necessary, even desirable. If you think of the ego as your true identity, you believe that giving it up would feel like dying.

Historically, institutions like the Church could convince you to dissolve your ego out of respect for the authority of organized religion, but the Church no longer commands that degree of influence. In the modern world, as our faith in institutions has eroded, we've come to recognize that moral authority must come from the individual. At the same time our awareness that we are part of a global community has been facilitated by technology, among other things. Our interconnectedness and the possibility of instantaneous communication can be used for good or for evil. Since there are no institutions that can convince everyone at once of the importance of choosing good over evil, it must happen on an individual basis, one person at a time. And therefore, it is a moment of awakening when a person recognizes that what choices they make do matter to humanity at large.

The idea that each one of us is aligned in a fundamental way with the spiritual condition of the universe makes everything we do and every choice we make more meaningful. When you act in congruence with the principles of the Higher World, it not only has a benefit to you and those around you, but it releases a force that mends the universe too.

This adds up to the fact that you can change the world. It doesn't matter who you are, what your status is, or how much you know. A clerk or bus driver is exactly as important as the CEO of a large company or the governor of your state. Your power comes from the *choices* you make. If you practice the tools and the attitudes we've discussed, you'll find yourself able to move from your Lower Self to your Higher Self, at will.

It's shocking to admit that the universe is "broken." It's sobering to know that only the human race can "put Humpty Dumpty back together again." Just "knowing" that won't give you the courage to accept this responsibility—you need to be inspired.

Don't wait around for inspiration to find you; go out and look for it. This is a new mind-set for most of us. We're used to seeing a world full of death, disharmony, and greed, a world where our deepest dreams seem impossible. But when you look between the cracks of dull, meaningless experience, you can always find the places where life breaks through and inspires you. You're left with a rising, bursting energy that has no limits.

When you're being carried by that wave, you'll find yourself able to put aside personal goals in the service of a higher mission. This state of selflessness makes you a better conduit. And as it does, you heal the world.

APPENDIX: THE TOOLS

The Black Sun

This tool can free you from one of Part X's most potent weapons—your own impulses.

DEPRIVATION: *Feel the deprivation of not getting what you want, as intensely as possible. Then let go of the thing you want. Forget about the outside world—let it disappear.*

EMPTINESS: *Look inside yourself. What was a feeling of deprivation is now an endless void. Face it. Remain calm and still.*

FULLNESS: *From the depths of the void, imagine a Black Sun ascends, expanding inside until you become one with its warm, limitless energy.*

GIVING: *Redirect your attention to the outside world. The Black Sun energy will overflow, surging out of you. As it enters the world, it becomes a pure, white light of infinite giving.*

The Vortex

This tool combats exhaustion and allows you to tap into boundless reserves of energy.

TWELVE SUNS: *See twelve suns in a circle lined up directly over your head. Summon the Vortex by silently screaming the word "help" with focused intensity. This will set the entire circle of suns spinning, creating a gentle tornado-shaped vortex.*

RISE: *Relax completely, allowing your body to become one with the vortex. Feel the pull of the vortex as it lifts you up through the circle of suns.*

GROW: *Once you're through the circle, feel yourself grow into a gentle giant with unlimited energy, moving slowly through the world without any resistance.*

The Mother

This tool dispels the negative thoughts that lead to demoralization, and replaces them with love and optimism.

TURN YOUR NEGATIVE THOUGHTS INTO A TOXIC SUBSTANCE: *Feel the sense of demoralization as intensely as you can. Focus on its heaviness, as if it's an oppressive substance weighing you down. Visualize that substance so vividly that the demoralized thoughts and feelings are no longer in your head.*

THE MOTHER APPEARS: *See the Mother hovering above you. Place your faith in her power to remove the dark, heavy substance* *you're holding on to. Let go of it. The Mother lifts it from your body as if it's weightless. Watch it rise until it reaches her; she absorbs it into herself and it disappears.*

FEEL HER LOVE: *Now feel her eyes upon you. They radiate absolute confidence in you; she believes in you unreservedly, like no one else ever has. With her unshakable faith filling you up, everything feels possible.*

The Tower

This tool transforms pain and hurt into strength, courage, and resilience.

DEATH: *Call up the hurt feelings that you just identified. Make them much worse and feel them attacking you right in your heart. They become so intense that your heart breaks and you die. You are left lying motionless on the ground.*

ILLUMINATION: *You hear a voice that says with great authority, "Only the dead survive." The moment it speaks, your heart fills with light, illuminating your surroundings. You see you are lying at the bottom of a hollow tower, which is open at the top. The light from your heart spreads through the rest of your body.*

TRANSCENDENCE: *Buoyed by the light, you effortlessly float up the tower and out the top, continuing your ascent into a perfect blue sky. Your body, purified of all pain, feels completely new.*

The Tools from our first book, *The Tools*
The Reversal of Desire

Use this tool when you need to take an action you have been avoiding. This tool connects you to the force of forward motion.

> **BRING IT ON:** *Focus on the pain you're avoiding; see it appear in front of you as a cloud. Silently scream, "Bring it on!" to demand the pain; you want it because it has great value.*

> **MOVE INTO THE PAIN CLOUD:** *Scream silently, "I love pain!" as you keep moving forward. Move so deeply into the pain you're at one with it.*

> **PAIN SETS YOU FREE:** *Feel the cloud spit you out and close behind you. Say inwardly, "Pain sets me free!" As you leave the cloud, feel yourself propelled forward into a realm of pure light.*

Active Love

Use this tool when you are consumed by obsessive anger—when you are trapped in the Maze. Active Love creates acceptance, freeing you so that you can give without reservation. You become unstoppable.

> **CONCENTRATION:** *Feel your heart expand to encompass the world of infinite love surrounding you. When your heart contracts back to normal size, it concentrates all this love inside your chest.*

> **TRANSMISSION:** *Send all the love from your chest to the other person, holding nothing back.*

PENETRATION: *When the love enters the other person, don't just watch, feel it enter; sense a oneness with him or her. Then relax, and you'll feel all the energy you gave away returned to you.*

Inner Authority

This tool allows you to overcome insecurity and be yourself.

SEE YOUR SHADOW: *Standing in front of any kind of audience, see your Shadow off to one side, facing you. (It works just as well with an imaginary audience or an audience composed of only one person.) Ignore the audience completely and focus all of your attention on the Shadow. Feel an unbreakable bond between the two of you—as a unit you're fearless.*

SPEAK WITH ONE VOICE: *Together, you and the Shadow forcefully turn toward the audience and silently command them to "LISTEN!" Feel the authority that comes when you and your Shadow speak with one voice.*

The Grateful Flow

Use this tool when your mind is filled with worry, self-hatred, or negative thinking. The tool connects you to a higher force of gratefulness that dissolves negativity.

LIST WHAT YOU'RE GRATEFUL FOR: *Start by silently stating to yourself specific things in your life you're grateful for, particularly items you'd normally take for granted. You can also include bad things that aren't happening. Go slowly so you really* feel *the gratefulness for each item. Don't use the same items each time you use the tool. You should feel a slight strain from having to come up with new ideas.*

FOCUS ON THE FEELING OF GRATEFULNESS: *Stop thinking and focus on the physical sensation of gratefulness. You'll feel it coming directly from your heart. This energy you are giving out is the Grateful Flow.*

CONNECT TO THE SOURCE: *As this energy emanates from your heart, your chest will soften and open. In this state, you will feel an overwhelming presence approach you, filled with the power of infinite giving. You've made a connection to the Source.*

Jeopardy

Use this tool when you need to summon willpower in order to keep using the tools.

See yourself lying on your deathbed. Having run out of time, this older self screams at you not to waste the present moment. You feel a deep, hidden fear that you've been squandering your life. This creates an urgent desire to use whichever basic tool you need at that moment.

ACKNOWLEDGMENTS

Foremost among the people I want to thank are my co-author and friend, Phil Stutz, and my wife, Judy White. This book could not have been written without their unwavering support. Phil is truly one of a kind—deep, wise, funny, and generous beyond anyone I've ever known. I am incredibly lucky to have met him. Likewise, it is virtually impossible to give adequate thanks to my wife. It's not easy to be married to someone who works all day, every day, and she has not only tolerated it without complaint, she has helped me tirelessly—with suggestions and encouragement—to reach ever higher. I love her with all my heart.

Both of my children inspire me. My daughter, Hana, is the funniest person I've ever met—always helping me laugh at myself and life's absurdities. My son, Jesse, burns with a Promethean fire—he inspires me to put my all into everything I do. I am so proud of the adults they have become.

Thanks also to a dedicated group of people who generously offered notes on our manuscript as it took shape. These include Debby Michels, David White, Bill Wheeler, and Maria Semple. Two more in this group deserve special thanks. Allison White rescued me from countless crises of confidence, keeping me sane whenever I started to spin out. And Nick Gillie eased me out of my comfort zone and introduced me to the courageous men and women of 2nd Call, in South Central Los Angeles, who showed me what Truth, Beauty, and Goodness look like in real life. Nick also told me the Reverend Lawson story which found its way into Chapter 7.

Finally, I would like to thank my patients. Every day I feel honored that you bare your souls and entrust your deepest secrets to me. The connections I've forged with you feel as close as any I've ever experienced. When I do battle with my own Part X, I remember the courage you show when you lift yourselves up—and it inspires me to fight harder. I could never be the person I am without you. Thank you for your faith in me, and for the very tangible help you've offered in bringing this book to fruition.

—Barry Michels

My profound thanks, as always, to my co-author, Barry Michels, who did more than his share in the execution of this book and did it with elegance and foresight. I am blessed to find a partner who loves the work we're doing as much as I do, or more. He's also the hardest worker I've ever seen.

I also want to thank the following people: Nick Gillie, who was instrumental in getting the book finished even though he doesn't realize it; Johanna Herwitz and Jamie Rose for their advice and energy; my parents, who—while no longer with us—seem smarter every day; Barbara McNally, who got me into writing in the first place. Maria Semple, who always told me the truth; Enid Ain, who has been a trusted colleague and friend for over forty years; Aline Garcia, my assistant and tireless one-woman support staff; Brian Johnson, who's been an enthusiastic and generous guide to getting our ideas out there.

Finally, to the late Brad Grey, one of the bravest human beings I've ever met.

—Phil Stutz

We'd like to thank the following people who, each in their own way, made it possible for this book to move from an idea to a reality. Their unshakable belief in our vision was a source of ceaseless encouragement and a guiding star that kept us on track. They gave freely of their time and effort every time we asked for it. These people are part of the heart and soul of the book: Julie Grau, our editor at Random House; Jennifer Rudolf Walsh, our agent; Jenn Brown, who helped with editing and organization; Brian Johnson, a tireless supporter of our work; and everyone at Goop.com who has championed our ideas. Finally, eternal thanks to Dana Goodyear, a supremely talented journalist who profiled our work in *The New Yorker* with a level of care and respect for which we'll be forever grateful.

—Barry Michels and Phil Stutz

STAY IN TOUCH

The Tools give you the power to change your life, but they won't work unless you actually *use* them. One of the best ways to maintain your motivation is to connect with the Tools community.

Sign up for the Tools email list at thetoolsbook.com.

- Get helpful articles, find out about upcoming events and workshops, and stay up to date on the latest from Barry, Phil, and the Tools community.

Join the closed Tools Group on Facebook: Facebook .com/groups/thetools.

- A lively community moderated by Tools coaches, this group offers support and guidance for those using the Tools in their daily lives.

Follow The Tools at Facebook.com/thetools and Twitter @TheToolsBook.

Email us at info@thetoolsbook.com.

About the Authors

BARRY MICHELS has a BA from Harvard, a law degree from University of California, Berkeley, and an MSW from the University of Southern California. He has been in private practice as a psychotherapist since 1986.

PHIL STUTZ graduated from City College in New York and received his MD from New York University. He worked as a prison psychiatrist on Rikers Island and then in private practice in New York before moving his practice to Los Angeles in 1982.

Visit the Tools website for more information and resources.

thetoolsbook.com